Menopause in Crisis—
The Summer I Lost My Mind

A memoir

Lynda Wyzda

Cover Design and Internal Formatting by *Scarlett Rugers Design;*

www.ScarlettRugers.com

Author Photo by Cynthia L. Starr

ISBN   13: 978-1492350552

           10: 1492350559

AUTHOR'S NOTE

This is a memoir about a "menopause in crisis" I experienced along with some of the events that led up to it the way I remember them. As memory can be a tricky sort of thing with the details of certain experiences being recalled differently by the various people involved, I realize that some individuals may have a different interpretation of what I've written here. Also, because conversations can be difficult to remember word for word, much of the dialogue I've included has been reconstructed; although I have made every effort to offer as close a representation of the actual exchanges as possible. The excerpts from the journal entries you'll find scattered throughout the memoir come directly from the journals I kept during the months of my crisis.

To my sons…
with immense love and gratitude.

"*Before the golden calm of Indian Summer*
come the long, wearying autumnal rains that beat the latest-
blooming chrysanthemums into the earth and despoil the trees of
their liveries of russet and purple.
A like 'change of life' falls upon the woman, one that renews the
memory of the unrest,
the mental perturbation and physical pains of the transition from
childhood to girlhood.
With some, the season is like the passage through the
Valley of the Shadow of Death…"

~~from *Eve's Daughters or Common Sense for Maid, Wife and Mother*
by Marion Harland, 1885

CONTENTS

A PREMONITION...

For the most part, I never saw my menopausal crisis coming. Sure, there were signs that I was heading for some sort of midlife breakdown and, to be honest, plenty of reasons why I should have had one as well. After all, I had arrived at this time of my life carrying so much extra baggage, emotional baggage that had been haunting me in one way or another for decades. Still, since I had managed to hold back any sort of serious undoing for this long, for nearly half a century, why would I think everything would suddenly start coming apart just because I was going through menopause? What was there to make me think this time of my life was going to be so different from any other?

Dream, from a few months before my crisis...

I'm driving along a country road in Columbia County, New York. It's a long, straight road with vast expanses of farmland stretching out in all directions. Off to the west, the Catskill Mountains rise up boldly into a cloud-cluttered sky. As I'm driving, I suddenly become aware of a tornado approaching—some ominous force of intense, swirling energy powerful enough to tear up everything within this peaceful scene and smash it to bits. Frightened, I stop my car and start running toward a group of nearby homes while several other people on the road do the same. After rushing inside one of the houses, a small white one, I hurry into the kitchen and start down the stairs into the basement. Just as I'm about to begin my descent, my left hand firmly on the railing, I turn to someone next to me and say, "As long as I'm able to survive, I can do this. I have to be here for my sons. My sons need me. I have to make it out alive for my sons…"

July

It was a night in mid-July 2005 around 2 a.m. when I woke up to use the bathroom. I have to admit, it was a pleasant surprise to discover I had been sleeping so soundly. So many other nights that summer the stirrings of menopause would not allow for that kind of luxury, wet pajamas and damp sheets waking me often into a chilly sweat. Truth be told, there had been countless other nights throughout my life when insomnia had me in such a tight grasp it was a struggle to get even an hour of sleep. Ah, but this night was different. This night, I was sleeping. But no sooner had I opened my eyes in those wee hours of that July night that I could sense I wasn't going to be going back to sleep anytime soon—some sort of shakiness inside… nervousness…something. Throwing off the covers, I hurried into the bathroom when, all of a sudden, I could feel my whole body beginning to shake: my arms, my legs, even my feet—my mind filling with wild and senseless fear. That's when the worst of it started.

Bam! Bam! Bam!

My heart began pounding so hard and so fast that I could feel it in nearly every cell of my body. Not knowing what to do, I ran out into the kitchen.

Bam! Bam! Bam!

What was happening? Was I having a heart attack? Was my heart about to explode? Since I'd already had plenty of panic attacks over the years, I knew right away that this was something much, much different. It was far more frantic than anything I'd experienced before, far more frantic and far more insistent.

Bam! Bam! Bam! BAM!

Something was wrong. Something was definitely wrong and getting worse with each terrifying "BAM" I could feel inside my chest. Alone with only my two fifteen year-old sons asleep in the house, I did something I never would have dreamed of doing before—I picked up the phone and dialed. In the middle of the night, the voice at the other end was a true comfort.

"911. What is the nature of your emergency?"

My mind racing, my hands shaking so violently I could hardly hold a glass of water, I tried to relate to the dispatcher the nature of my emergency, an emergency I could neither identify nor explain.

"M…m…my heart is pounding. A…a…and my hands are shaking…my whole body is shaking. I think it must be something I ate…the meat…something."

"Do you want us to send an ambulance?" the dispatcher asked.

I hesitated, stalled, all the while struggling to figure out what I should do next.

What do I do? I thought, clinging to the phone. *My heart is beating so fast! What do I do?*

Not wanting to frighten my sons with ambulances and late-night sirens, I finally decided not to have the paramedics come and, instead, to try and tough it out alone. With a husband who spent much of his time traveling for business, I was used to toughing things out alone and figured, once I was able to pull myself together, I'd be able to manage this as well.

So, after gathering all the consolation I could from the dispatcher, I took a deep, shaky breath and reluctantly hung up the phone. By this time, the pounding in my chest had begun to slow into a somewhat more familiar pulse, and although the shaking was still there, that too seemed to be subsiding. Still dazed, I crawled back into bed, armed with a glass of water and high hopes that the episode had passed. Hopes that were all too quickly dashed as the instant I tried to lie down, the instant I tried to lay my head on the pillow so I could get some rest, my body became filled with feelings of such haunting agitation, I couldn't lay still. Again and again, I changed my position, and, again and again, the agitation, the intense restlessness returned. It was as if an explosion had occurred inside me and now all the little pieces of debris were floating around inside my body, looking for a place to land or be released. Finally, after stacking enough pillows under my head to make my body more vertical than horizontal, I curled up into the tightest fetal position I could, closed my eyes, and did my best to go back to sleep, only managing to doze off for a few minutes before the buzz of the alarm told me it was morning.

****

Never before that night would I have thought that menopause, or more specifically perimenopause (the eight or so years before a woman's menstrual cycles cease) could bring on such intense bodily symptoms. Actually, what I believed about The Change was that I'd simply sweat a few times, change my pj's once or twice, and then be done with the whole process. Since I'd been having some pretty intense hot flashes and night sweats in the weeks before my episode, however, I couldn't help but wonder if the two events could be related. Ever the consummate researcher, the next day I sat down at my computer, logged onto the internet and typed the words "perimenopause and night panic" into the search engine. I don't think I really expected to find anything but figured a few minutes of web surfing was worth the effort of trying to put my mind and body at ease. I could hardly believe my eyes when, with one small click of the mouse, not just one but several websites came up, one that astounded me. On the website, I discovered pages and pages of posts where dozens of other women were writing about their experiences with perimenopausal night terror and panic, about their middle-of-the-night trips to the emergency room, and the various dosages of Xanax many of them needed to get through the night.

Oh, my gosh, I thought. *If it's only perimenopause, I'll be fine. I'll be ready for it the next time and won't let it throw me off kilter so much.*

I was so relieved to learn that my middle-of-the-night panic was nothing more than a normal symptom of perimenopause that I even started joking about it later that afternoon with my sons.

"Hey, could you imagine someone a little more high strung like your aunt having one of these episodes?" I chucked. "She'd be running around the house in a panic screaming, 'Oh, my God! Oh, my God!'"

Unfortunately, that hilarious moment of heckling didn't last long. A few days later, I was on my way home after dropping my sons off at drama camp. It was a warm, sunny day so I had the car windows open and was actually whistling, certain I had this whole perimenopause thing under control. All in all, I was feeling quite pleased with myself when, all of a sudden—

Bam! Bam! Bam!

Determined not to panic this time, I held tight to the steering wheel and pulled into a nearby diner.

Bam! Bam! Bam!

Relax, I thought to myself. *It's only perimenopause!*

Hands shaking and mind reeling, I reached into my purse, took out my cell phone and put it in the cup holder, just in case I did need to call the paramedics.

Bam! Bam! Bam! BAM!

Come on, Lynda…steady now! Breathe…Breathe!

But no matter how hard I tried to relax, no matter how hard I tried to calm myself down with some of the relaxation techniques I'd learned in my yoga training, the pounding would not let up, the pounding or the panic. As I sat there, wondering what to do next, deep inside I could feel wave after wave of monstrous terror welling up from some far away time and place, each one threatening to wash me away in the undertow.

Should I call the hospital? I wondered, my hand already on the cell phone. *Oh, my God! Oh, my God!*

FEMININE FORCES

Power-surge.com. That's the website where I discovered
the posts written by the many women who were also battling
episodes of panic during perimenopause, especially night panic.
As I read through some of what they had written, I was amazed
to see how many of these women had also called the emergency
room during these episodes, and even more astounded by the
number who had actually gone there, a few more than once.
Although I truly empathized with what these women were
going through, it was a comfort for me to learn that I was not
alone in my struggle. From what I was able to gather from
the website, what each of these women was experiencing was
nothing more than a normal manifestation of shifting feminine
hormones, something both they and I would, most likely, just
have to deal with. But even in that moment of relief, that
moment of blessed, bodily relief, I couldn't help wondering
why only some of the women on the website were having
these types of experiences. Why was it that only some women
were finding themselves leveled by feelings of fear, anxiety, and
panic while others seemed to be soaring through The Change

with little more than an occasional hot flash? Somewhere along the line, through the grapevine of "Old Wives' Tales" I suppose, I could remember hearing that it was usually women who'd had a difficult time with Premenstrual Syndrome or PMS who would also wind up struggling through a difficult perimenopause—that, somehow, the two were related. This got me thinking. Could this have been what was behind my own recent attacks of night panic and panic while driving? Could these perimenopausal difficulties have been related in some way to my earlier struggles with PMS as well as some of my other feminine challenges, my feminine "disturbances"?

Looking back, I could remember how it was only a few months after I started menstruating at just nine years-old that I began to feel like I was fighting a losing battle with PMS. Every few weeks, it felt as if my mind and body were being assaulted by some strange alien force as I struggled to make my way through the barrage of premenstrual challenges that had suddenly taken over my life, challenges that included weight gain, acne, swollen breasts, sleeplessness, anxiety, feelings of self-loathing, and, of course, those cursed cramps.

I can recall now how, still wearing my princess pajamas, I used to curl up on the living room sofa each month as soon as my period would begin, some days barely able to move from the cramps. One morning, I think it was when I was twelve or thirteen years-old, I decided to try going to my guitar lesson during one of these assaults. As I labored to make my way through the difficult classical piece, I could feel that familiar twisting, that tugging in my lower abdomen, cramps so strong I could hardly hold the guitar.

"I think we should stop," my guitar teacher said. He was an older man, old and stern and not normally one to stray outside the lines. "You look green," he continued. "You must have the flu or something. I think you should go on home."

Although I did leave my lesson early that day, I was in so much pain that I wasn't able to tolerate the twenty-minute drive back to my house. Instead, I sat hunched over on a toilet in some gas station restroom, clutching my stomach and waiting for the cramps to pass. As difficult as the physical symptoms were—the cramps, the bloating, the swollen breasts—it was the emotional symptoms, the self-loathing that always caused me the most pain.

"I don't think I can go on like this," I can remember crying to my mother one afternoon, my mind and body racked with the wiles of PMS. "If I have to, I'm afraid I might wind up killing myself."

It was just a few months after this painful disclosure that yet another "disturbance" began to descend on my adolescence, one that, for me, seemed to also be connected to my feminine processes—anorexia nervosa. Only during the mid-1970's, there didn't seem to be a name for this self-inflicted act of starvation, or at least none that my doctors were aware of. I was an anomaly of sorts, or, given the way the number of cases of anorexia has since exploded in our culture, perhaps it was more that I was some sort of pioneer. There weren't any self-help books back then that I could read to try to find out why I so needed to starve myself, and no blog or support group I could turn to for answers. Back then, there was only me, my calorie-counting handbook, and those numbers on the scale.

At 5'7" tall, I weighed in at 129 pounds that April of 1975. All I wanted to do was get down to 125, so I stopped eating candy whenever I went to the movies and cookies while at home. It seemed like a simple enough plan, a healthy one too.

After seeing my weight actually drop after a few weeks of this determined effort, I felt inspired...powerful, and so set out to lose even more weight. Since I hadn't seen the number "120" on the scale for so long, probably since middle school, I next set my sights there. Wow! I could hardly believe it! Another success! It was as if I had entered some kind of contest and was winning every event—except, the only person in the contest, the only person to beat, was me. In time, I became so obsessed with dieting and losing weight that it got to where my health and the way I looked didn't even matter. After just a few weeks of subsisting on little more than a few egg whites and a couple of stalks of broccoli each day, and maybe a dab of mustard, my hair became noticeably brittle, my skin uncomfortably dry, and my body so thin that people started calling me "Bones."

"Eew, that's disgusting," I can remember a friend of mine squealing after she grabbed hold of my arm one morning and noticed how scrawny it was.

"It looks like your acne has cleared up," I can remember another friend commenting. "Now if only you could gain some weight."

Although these outer changes certainly were alarming, there were also inner changes that came with the weight loss, changes no one could see like dizziness, near fainting spells, and, most unsettling, the loss of my menstrual cycles. One month, I started bleeding the way I always did, and then the next month, there was nothing. Days passed, then weeks, and still no period. Although my mother did take me to see a gynecologist a few times, first to see if I might be pregnant and then to try and bring on a period through a series of hormone injections, the loss of my cycles didn't concern me. To me, the only thing that mattered was how much weight I was losing, and how much

more I could lose if I could only stop eating. After all, as long
as I wasn't having periods, there would be no more PMS, no
more bloating, swollen breasts, or cramps. Ah, but would I ever
be able to escape the self-loathing?

It wasn't until I discovered long-distance running just after
I turned nineteen that I was able to escape the self-loathing
enough to move forward with my life. Running up to sixty-five
miles a week had my endorphins through the roof and enough
calories burning that I didn't have to fear eating so much. In
time, I managed to regain all of the weight I'd lost during my
stint of starvation, and was even able to add a few extra pounds
of muscle. Later, when my PMS began to return along with
my menstrual cycles, I discovered natural progesterone cream
as a way of alleviating some of my more severe premenstrual
challenges, especially the ones that were affecting my running
like bloating and weight gain. After a few years of solo running
and road racing, I met another distance runner and soon we
were married and running in races together. Although it
did take some careful timing on my part, when I was thirty
I became pregnant, and, since my body was already so used
to it, was able to keep right on running for several months
as my belly grew and my mind filled with thoughts of babies
and motherhood. Finally, on a warm, sunny day in the spring
of 1990, I gave birth to healthy identical twin boys, each of
them weighing in at exactly 6 ¾ pounds, and who I decided to
name David and Jonathan long before my labor even began.
A month or so after my sons were born, I bought a jogging
stroller, and, before long, there were four of us out on the road
each morning—my sons, my wire-haired terrier, and me. I was
at the top of my game, running and enjoying my new life as

a mother. From the outside, things couldn't have been better. Underneath this calm, however, this happy and carefree life, I could still feel the old "disturbances" tugging at my sleeve as well as a few new ones beginning to emerge.

It was before I even became pregnant that I noticed I was beginning to have a hard time talking to people, an especially hard time. It seemed that nearly every time I opened my mouth to try to say something, my face would turn red, I'd break out in a sweat, and feel like I was going to cry. No matter how hard I tried to contain these surges, to look away or think about something else, there was nothing I could do to stop them. In fact, the harder I tried to stop them, the worse they'd become. Once I was able to get through one of these episodes and would be sitting alone in my room, I'd try to figure out what it was I was feeling when my face started to turn red, but the only emotion I could come up with was shame—simple and timeless shame. But where was this shame coming from? What could I have possibly been so ashamed of that I could barely speak?

It was around this same time, during my late twenties, that I also began to experience another unnerving "disturbance"— heart palpitations, episodes where there didn't seem to be any rhythm at all to my heart rate, just some frantic flip-flopping inside my chest.

Thump…thump, thump…flutter…flutter, thump…Ka-THUNK!

Almost overnight, these palpitations became so frequent and so intense that I decided I should see a doctor to try to find out what was causing them. After running an ultrasound and a stress test, the cardiologist concluded that the palpitations weren't anything to worry about and told me I could go on with my normal activities. And yet, even as I continued with my running, and later with my life as a mother, as with the PMS and "surges of shame," my palpitations continued to worsen.

It was as I was approaching my mid-forties that one of my most frustrating and persistent "disturbances" suddenly reappeared—struggles with food. Only now, it wasn't an unwillingness to eat that kept me away from the table but an inability to do so because of what appeared to be food allergies.

The first food to affect me was my morning bowl of wheat cereal, a breakfast I'd been enjoying for years but which suddenly began giving me severe cases of brain fog. After a few weeks, anything with even the slightest bit of wheat or gluten in it began to bother me, and then, anything at all made with grains. By this time, it wasn't just brain fog that these foods were causing either, but a sensation that felt as if I had burned my tongue on something, and, even more worrisome, a racing heart and skyrocketing blood pressure.

"That's the kind of thing that can kill you," I can remember my doctor saying after I told her about my pulse and blood pressure. "You'll want to be especially careful with that."

As I continued to develop more and more bizarre reactions to foods, I began dropping more and more of them out of my diet—first dairy products and soy, then wheat products and grains, and finally, even most fruits. Although I'd been a vegetarian and vegan for most of my life, not knowing what else to do, I soon decided to put meat back into my diet, thinking it was more protein I needed. By the beginning of July, it seemed that all I was eating was organic lamb and macadamia nuts, jars and jars of macadamia nuts. Then, once those foods started causing reactions, it was nothing but sweet potatoes and quinoa, and, before long, nothing but turnips and broccoli. Night after night, I would cook regular food for my sons, things like spaghetti and meatballs, lasagna, or chicken curry, and then go off and cook something else for myself—lamb and quinoa, turnips and broccoli. All in all, this would have been fine except every time I was able to find something I could eat without causing my heart to race, it would last only for a few days, sometimes even only a few hours. Before I knew it, my heart would start pounding all over again, and I'd be right back to trying to figure out which other food I should omit from my already dwindling daily fare. I can remember just before the bottom dropped out in July, standing in the middle of my kitchen, frantic and frustrated and thinking to myself—

There's nothing left that I can eat. What am I going to do now?

Well, from what I'd been reading on the website for Power Surge, it seemed that now I was entering perimenopause, a time when I could expect any number of new feminine challenges to enter my life, challenges like the night panic I was already becoming well acquainted with. Wanting to know more about these types of challenges as well as what other surprises awaited me during this time of hormonal shift, I began searching the internet for other menopause-related websites. At some point, I stumbled across one that offered a whole list of the various physical and emotional challenges a woman could expect to encounter during The Change. At the time, this list included thirty-four menopausal challenges or symptoms, seven of which seemed to leap out at me from the page:

-Difficulty concentrating, disorientation, mental confusion
  -Sleep disturbances, with or without night sweats
  -Bouts of rapid heart beat
  -Anxiety, feeling ill at ease
  -Panic disorder
  -Increased allergies
  -Burning tongue

I was so comforted by how this list seemed to include every "disturbance" I was experiencing that I decided to print it out so I could refer to it anytime I needed reassurance that everything I was going through was perfectly normal. After all, perimenopause is a natural life transition, a transition that, whether mild or severe, all women go through once they reach midlife—a transition I felt certain I'd already seen the worst of.

August

Although I did manage to drive home from the diner that day without calling the paramedics, this time the pounding in my chest did not subside. In fact, over the next few weeks all of my "disturbances" began to worsen. By the first week of August, my pulse, which was usually around sixty-five or so, had begun to race not only after I ate but all throughout the day and night, now pounding at a constant eighty-five to ninety beats per minute. My blood pressure, which was normally about 110/65, had also begun to skyrocket around the clock, most often to around 145/90 but sometimes climbing even higher. I was so frightened by these changes, by how sudden and drastic they were, that I began checking my vital signs over and over again, terrified by how high the numbers might be the next time I checked them, and the next time, and the next time, and the next time after that.

Within just a few days of this nervous and frantic checking, I found myself starting to feel confused, confused and anxious, so anxious that my whole body began to tremble, and then to shake. Or, was it the shaking that caused the anxiousness and the anxiousness that caused the confusion? Everything was falling apart so quickly. There was no way for me to know what was causing what or which "disturbance" had come before all the others. Although I did try to keep reassuring myself with my list of "The 34 Menopause Symptoms" that everything I was experiencing was perfectly normal, as the chaos inside my body continued to worsen it became more and more difficult for me to believe that something as simple as perimenopause could be causing it.

There's no way this can all be from perimenopause, I thought, trying to keep myself from shaking. *No way.*

Thinking that it might be my long standing issues with low blood sugar causing my "disturbances," during the first week of August I decided to cut all carbohydrates out of my diet— everything—right down to the simplest of starchy vegetables. Noticing that this seemed to make my "disturbances" worse rather than better, I went out and bought myself a glucose monitor and began pricking my finger to test my blood sugar, not just once or twice a day as recommended but twenty and thirty times a day, sometimes taking ten readings at one sitting.

"What's happening to me?" I'd moan as I'd start pricking my finger for the eighth or ninth time in a row. "Oh, my God, what's happening to me?"

Whatever was happening, it was obvious that along with the chaos that had erupted in my body, an even more frightening chaos was erupting in my mind, and no matter what I did—no matter what changes I made to my diet, to my sleep schedule, or to any other aspect of my daily routine—there was nothing I could do to stop it.

****

Journal Entry 8/6/05

> "...*So sick...so awfully, awfully sick. Couldn't figure out why every time I ate yesterday, I'd feel worse. I had a tablespoon—just a tablespoon of cottage cheese and from there it's been hell. Every time I put something in my mouth it seemed I'd react. What the hell? Can I just not eat anymore? The buffalo, the lamb, even the chicken all seem to make me so terribly, terribly anxious. Just don't want to eat anymore—now how awful is that?"*

Even when I went to bed, I could find no rest from this constant struggle with anxiety and food as all throughout the night, I'd find myself waking up again and again, sweating and shaking and feeling like I needed to eat something. It didn't matter that it was still only two or three o'clock in the morning. I'd wake up with such fear and trembling that as soon as I opened my eyes, I'd run out to the kitchen and start checking my blood sugar—once, twice, three times, four times, five. Then I'd try eating something in the hopes of getting my blood sugar up high enough to be able to go back to sleep, only to find myself being kept awake by some other food reaction or by my heart's relentless pounding. Even on the nights I was able to fall back to sleep, within the hour the whole process would start all over again, and I'd be right back out in the kitchen, pricking my finger and eating, pricking my finger and eating.

Before I could figure out what was going on with my blood sugar, lo and behold, another "disturbance" appeared—this one difficulty swallowing. Although this was something I'd always had some trouble with when eating certain foods, by August there were times I couldn't swallow at all. I can remember one late night, getting out of bed to drink a glass of water. The house was dark, and I could see the stars glistening in the sky outside my window as I lifted the glass up to my mouth. The instant that first sip of clear, cool water slipped past my lips, however, I could feel the muscles in my throat suddenly slam shut.

Slam!

It was as if they had become paralyzed, or that they had forgotten the mechanism for swallowing, or maybe…maybe it was that they simply refused to swallow.

Why? I wondered. *Why won't my throat muscles let me swallow?*

From that night on, trying to get the sweet potatoes down, the turnips, the broccoli, every mouthful was a struggle and took my total concentration to keep from choking. Many nights, I'd find myself sitting at the dinner table, coughing and gasping for air, all the while with my sons sitting across from me asking again and again if I was alright.

"Mom! Mom! Are you okay?"

"Mom!"

Before long, I became afraid to eat anything at all, afraid that either the pounding in my chest or the choking was going to kill me.

As I continued my battle with my racing heart and skyrocketing blood pressure, with my difficulty swallowing and myriad of food allergies, I soon noticed yet another "disturbance" rising out of the fray. It was a "disturbance" I couldn't remember having before that summer and which didn't seem to be in any way related to food, something I came to refer to in my daily journal entries as the "twitch thing."

Although the "twitch thing" may have been occurring on some level at other times of the day without my being aware of it, I only noticed it when I was lying in *Svasana* or Final Relaxation at the end of my daily yoga practice. While this posture would normally lead me to a place of deep relaxation and ease, by the beginning of August, it was leading me to a place of sheer torment. The instant I'd feel myself starting to relax, the instant I'd feel myself drifting off to that peaceful, meditative state, there'd be a sudden whooshing inside my brain, a feeling of pressure, and then a sensation that felt as if I were being pulled underwater—just for a moment, everything turning all slow-motioned and surreal before plunging me back into yet another rapid-pulsed, skyrocketing blood pressure frenzy. Some days, at the very first sign of the "twitch thing," I'd leap up off the floor and start checking my vital signs.

Pulse—92! Blood pressure—157/88! What's wrong with me? Oh, God, what's wrong with me?

Other days, I'd stay put on the floor and do my best to try to understand where the "twitch thing" was coming from and what it wanted from me. But no matter how hard I tried to figure the "twitch thing" out, I could make no sense of it, no sense beyond the sinking, the tearing, and the sudden blood pressure rush.

Given all of the chaos that was erupting inside my body, it was getting to where I was hardly able to get any sleep at all. I'd sleep an hour here and an hour there, but nowhere near enough to give my frenzied body the rest it needed. Even in the brief intervals of sleep I was able to get, more often than not, I'd find myself being startled awake by yet another "disturbance"—a feeling I can best describe as electric jolts racing through my body.

Zsst, zsst. Zap, zap…zap.

There were nights when these "zssts" and "zaps" would electrify me so fully that, whether sound asleep or wide-awake, I'd sometimes feel myself being yanked up into a sitting position by some force that seemed beyond my conscious control. These jolts were so powerful and so forceful at times that had I been of a different mindset, I might have thought them to be the result of some sort of otherworldly possession. Given my long-standing struggles with food, however, to me these jolts could mean only one thing—another drop in blood sugar. So, off to the kitchen I'd go for yet another finger prick and yet another bowl of turnips, still struggling, *always* struggling to swallow. I can remember some nights feeling so disoriented during these late-night treks to the kitchen that I'd wind up sitting on the cold, linoleum floor with my hands pressed up against my head while peering into the lower cabinets—looking at the potatoes, looking at the cooking oil, looking, I suppose, for some shred of my sanity.

As frightening as all of these physical changes were, frightening and chaotic, they weren't the only "disturbances" following me into that cursed vortex, chasing me there. Within every moment of all of my other strange bodily happenings, I'd also begun to notice this smell, this odor, an overwhelming stench that soon began hounding and haunting me through every second of my already deeply disturbed days and nights.

Is it my lipstick? I'd wonder as I pressed the tube of "Blushing Beige" up against my nose. *Is it my deodorant? My shampoo? Is it me?*

But even though hardly a moment would pass without that hideous smell wafting up from someplace deep inside me, I could smell nothing, nothing from the world outside me—not my lipstick, my deodorant or my shampoo, not even the onions I would chop for dinner, and, most alarming, not even the eye-watering stench of a skunk...

It happened one early evening in the middle of August while I was outside walking my dog. Ever the curious creature, she went and got herself sprayed by a skunk. I knew this. I had heard the scuffle in the bushes and managed to see the helpless look of repulsion on the poor dog's face as she emerged from the thicket, and yet, for some reason, I couldn't smell it. No matter how deeply I inhaled the moist evening air into my nose, I couldn't smell the skunk, not a single whiff of its angry and frightened retaliation. When I got home, I could see that my sons were just as repulsed by the smell as my dog as they hurried away from her and lamented to me from across the kitchen—

"Oh, my God! Mom, we'd better give the dog a bath!"

What's wrong with me? I wondered as I sniffed at the dog's fur. *Why can't I smell anything? Why can't I even smell the skunk?*

We did decide to give the dog a bath that night and although I was feeling far more repulsed than anyone else in my house—my sons or my dog—my repulsion didn't have anything to do with the skunk. It was from an odor only I could smell.

****

Even before my sons learned to read, they always loved going to libraries and bookstores, especially bookstores that sold used books. I think it was something about the older books,

books from my day that they so enjoyed looking at—sort of like ancient treasure hiding in between the stacks. Having recently learned of just such a bookstore in a nearby town, David and Jonathan asked if we could go and see what we could find there. Since things had been so shaky at home recently because of my "disturbances," I thought it would be a good idea if we tried to do something normal for a change, so despite my ongoing issues with panic while driving, I agreed to take them. Fortunately, we planned our outing for August 12th, a day that, according to my journal entries, I woke up feeling refreshed and well rested.

Journal Entry 8/12/05
    "I Slept! I Slept! I Slept! I Slept! I Slept! And only woke up at 2:30 and 6:30 for food. Still starving, I must admit. Absolutely ravenous and so looking forward to hopefully a few calm weeks before menopause/PMS hit again..."

Feeling somewhat renewed by this night of restful sleep, sometime in the late morning or early afternoon I got into the car with my sons and headed for the bookstore. Being as wrapped up as many people were at that time in the adventures of Harry Potter, in addition to reading the books we had also taken up listening to the audio versions of the stories, enraptured by the voice talents of Jim Dale as he skillfully brought each character to life. Since we would be in the car for at least a half an hour before arriving at our destination, my sons decided to put one of the Harry Potter tapes into the cassette player to brighten up our trip. It was after only about ten minutes or so of trying to drive and listen to the tape that I found myself plummeting into a whole new "disturbance"—no matter how hard I tried, I couldn't understand anything that was being said on the tape, not a single word. I could tell that there were words coming out of the speakers, a whole slew of them, but, somehow, they all sounded jumbled, out of order, as if they were all floating around un-manned in space. I didn't want to say anything to my sons about what was happening, nor could I even if I had wanted to. For the life of me, I didn't know what was happening. I didn't understand it and was far too terrified to try. Finally, after another ten minutes or so of trying to drive while listening to those confused mutterings, I asked my sons if we could turn the tape off for a while so I could think. Although, to be honest, by this time thinking had become just as confusing for me, my thoughts often more jumbled than the words on the tape. Was I going crazy? Was that what was happening to me? And, if I was, how was I going to explain that to my sons?

Journal Entry 8/15/05

   "...Dreadful day and night—had some kind of reaction to I think the new olive oil I bought—pounding heart, anxiety to beat the band. Awful. Tried the buffered vitamin C—worked after a while but then I think it kept me up last night. Either that or I'm hyperthyroid—but then why would I have felt so good day before yesterday? What's happening to me? I'm so scared, so scared and no one to help...can't seem to get any sleep except these few nights. Rather have the hot flashes than this any day...Feel so bad for the boys too, having to put up with all of this. It's too much now, too much for too long..."

****

Throughout the years before perimenopause, I rarely saw my doctor for anything other than my annual physical. Even when I nearly cut the tip of my finger off with the rose clipper one summer, all I did was slap a butterfly-bandage on the severed piece of flesh and then went on about my business—only to find myself being chastised by my doctor a few days later about how important it is to get stitches for this type of wound. Now, however, with my "disturbances" growing worse by the day, I soon began seeing my doctor on a near-daily basis. Several times a week this doctor would come out of her office to find me curled up on a chair inside her waiting room—trembling, thin, and pale.

"Are you feeling any better?" the doctor would ask.

"No…no," I'd answer, my mind awash with panic. "No. In fact, I feel worse."

In an effort to come up with a diagnosis for my condition, this compassionate doctor went ahead and ran every test she could think of—tests for Lyme Disease and hyperthyroid, for Ehrlichiosis and Babesiosis, and even for liver disease. When these tests didn't reveal anything, she went back, tested my hemoglobin and platelet count and then went on to check my cholesterol. But nothing could explain my symptoms. According to the tests, I was a healthy forty-six year-old woman. So, why did my body feel like it was falling apart?

Because of all the food reactions I'd been having, one thing my doctor did think might be a good idea was if I went to see an allergist, her hope being that if I could find out exactly what foods were causing my "disturbances," I could eliminate them and start to feel some relief. After talking to the allergist on the phone, I found that he too thought I might have a few food allergies, so I went ahead and made an appointment to have some blood tests. Several days after the tests were finished, anxious to adjust my diet and get on with my life, I called the allergist's office for the results.

"The tests are all negative," the nurse said after I gave her my name.

"What?" I asked nervously. "I don't understand."

"You don't have any food allergies at all," the nurse said to clarify. "Everything came up negative."

I can remember that sinking feeling in my stomach as I began to realize exactly what the nurse was saying and what that meant about my "disturbances." Every food I'd been tested for had come up negative, dozens of foods: milk, eggs, wheat, soy, plums, peaches, even the most notorious of all allergy-causing foods—peanuts. According to the tests, I had no food allergies whatsoever. None. So, what was causing my "disturbances"? Every time I tried to eat anything, anything at all, my heart would start pounding. My heart would start pounding and each time it did, I could feel it slamming up against the inside of my chest like some caged animal, like some wild beast, desperate for release. It got so bad that I started holding my hand to my chest most of the time, while driving, while sitting in the doctor's office, and even while sitting in front of my computer searching for a website that could explain what was happening to me. My intention, my *mission*, I presume, was to hold the beast inside.

****

The summer continued to swelter and slip across the sky, slowly making room for the season waiting in the wings. And as the shadows began to lengthen, I began having my suspicions as to what besides perimenopause and low blood sugar might be causing my "disturbances." In a desperate attempt to regain a hold of my life, on August 16th I decided to call my mother. At that time, I hadn't spoken to her for several months, and, before that hiatus, had once let several years pass incommunicado until the day my father died in 2002—coincidentally on August 15th, 2002, slipping out of his nursing home bed at the age of seventy-one on the wings of severe alcoholic dementia. My father—the last four years of his life spent strapped to his bed or wheelchair, feeding-tubed and diapered and with barely a clue as to who he or I was. It was the culmination of a life kept afloat by literally hundreds of gallons of gin, something that for him seemed to be the only way of dealing with everything that had gone wrong in our family. You see, when I called my mother that afternoon, I did so to talk to her about the sexual abuse, about the incest I had begun to remember several years earlier, in 1993, within the tailspin of another dream…

I'm standing in the kitchen of my childhood home, doing everything I can to shut the back door, my mother standing next to me, to my right. With all my strength, I keep pushing and pushing but still can't get the door to close. On the other side of the door, I can see nothing but a thick, heavy blackness, the very blackness I seem to be fighting. My arms growing weary from pushing, I keep trying to shut the door, but no matter what I do, it keeps opening. As I'm waking up from the dream, I can hear myself crying out, "Get off of me, Dad! Get off of me!"

Since the man I was living with at the time was there next to me when I had this dream, a man who would later become my second husband, my husband during my crisis, even if I had wanted to there wasn't any way I could ignore the words I had spoken or the images from my dream.

"What happened?" my friend asked the instant I opened my eyes. "What were you dreaming?"

As I began telling my friend about the dream, I found myself experiencing feelings I used to have at night as a child, feelings that everything in my room was becoming larger than it should be, larger and heavier and all of it moving in slow motion. As I tried to demonstrate this heaviness for my friend with the sheets, lifting the sheets with my hands, I began to cry, and sweat, and shake, my entire body re-entering the terror of those slow-motioned nights.

"Did your father rape you?" my friend asked.

Still clinging to the sheets, I searched my mind for an answer, every corner of my mind, but was unable to find one. I had no memory of this…this…this rape, only of the fear and of the suffocating darkness.

Poem written in 2001—

Half asleep, Izzy reached for her doll.
It was too dark to see but with tender fingers
she could tell that the doll's eyes were wide open and staring.
Something had frightened her.
In the still, humid night,
something had frightened her.
Izzy knew because she was frightened as well.
All around the little girl room,

around its ruffles and its lace,
the darkness seemed to be taking on life and form,
the air so heavy and thick Izzy thought for sure it would crush her.
It hovered above the bed only for a moment then heaved.

Hardly breathing.
Hardly breathing.

Even the sheets felt heavy as Izzy struggled beneath them,
struggled for air,
struggled for light and cold.
But there would be no release,
not on this night,
for on this night
the monster had returned.

As I wrestled to come to terms with the meaning behind my dream, behind the door and the darkness, I could remember a day several months earlier when I overheard my parents' arguing, my father insisting that I needed to go to a psychiatric hospital for help and my mother unconvinced.

"Why?" my mother demanded. "Why do you think Lynda needs to go to the hospital?"

I could hear my father's voice come back deliberate and slow, hauntingly sober.

"Because she had a bad father," he said sadly. "Because she had a bad father."

It would take several years and many more dreams and incidents of returning memory before I would finally be able to trust the message these nighttime images were trying to convey, and to begin to accept the fact that yes, I'd been molested—the fact that yes…yes, I'd been raped.

In a desperate effort to save my sanity that August afternoon, I called my mother and while we were on the phone, tried to explain to her how much the sexual abuse had affected me, how much it hurt me. (Or was I trying to explain this more to myself?) As with my dream, again, I found myself trembling, and sobbing, and sweating, so much so that by the time I hung up the phone an hour later, my blood sugar had slipped to one of its lowest points ever. I was a mess, an absolute wreck, and yet, at the same time, I couldn't help but feel ecstatic. After so many years of trying to hold the door shut, of trying to keep the truth of my childhood inside, I'd finally found the courage to open the door and let the truth go free. Not wanting my sons to get caught in the backdraft of my tears and telephone tirades, my sobbing and shaking, I thought it was time I told them about my abuse as well.

"I just wanted to make sure you guys know what's been going on," I said. "That it was me I was writing about in all those poems and short stories about sexual abuse, that I'm the one who was molested. You know that, right?"

"Yeah, Mom," David and Jonathan said solemnly. "Sure. Of course we do."

I was so excited to have finally gotten my past out into the open with everyone in my life that on my way outside later that afternoon, I actually threw my arms out to my sides and let out a cry of glee. After speaking with my mother about my abuse, I felt one-hundred percent certain that it was this truth, a truth that had been locked away inside of me for decades, that was the very beast that had been causing my "disturbances." Now that I had released this beast, my "disturbances" were bound to disappear. Finally, I'd be able to eat! Finally, I'd be able to sleep!

Not so fast, whispered the beast. *Not so fast.*

Much to my horror, later that night I found myself spiraling into an even wilder state of chaos.

Journal Entry 8/17/05

> *"....didn't sleep last night. My blood sugar was plummeting every hour...I told my mother about my abuse. I shouldn't even have called—should have worked to keep myself on an even keel but noooo...At first I thought this was a great thing—getting that out in the open—now I'm not so sure. Not so sure at all. I feel awful—no sleep, blood sugar a mess...Please, oh please help me...someone. Why can't I heal?"*

****

Still certain that my struggles were at least in some way related to perimenopause, each time I saw my doctor that August I asked for bio-identical hormones, and each time I asked, she refused. It would take several of these confrontations before I finally learned that this doctor, a woman who was in her late-fifties at the time, was already taking estrogen for her own perimenopausal difficulties.

"My gynecologist says it's going to kill me," my doctor confessed to me one afternoon. "She says it's going to kill me, but every time I try to go off of it my blood pressure spikes and I get this awful anxiety. I even went to the emergency room once. You don't want to take estrogen," she said emphatically. "Don't even get started."

Knowing a little bit about my abuse from what I had told her a few months earlier, my doctor then looked at me and said something which, because of how terrified I was about my physical "disturbances," I wasn't able to fully grasp until several years later.

"You have a lot of emotional baggage," she said, her brown eyes refusing to release my gaze. "…*a lot* of emotional baggage."

****

In addition to all of the medical appointments that I had been making for myself that August, I'd also made an appointment for my sons to see their doctor so that they could have their annual physicals. I had known this doctor for several years and had wanted to talk to him for some time about the stress my sons had been under, stress caused by the usual adolescent school and dating issues, yes, but mostly the stress caused by my perimenopausal "disturbances." I was hoping this doctor might be able to offer me some advice regarding counseling for my sons, and maybe even a little advice about menopause as well.

"Wow, two teenage boys *and* you're going through menopause," the doctor commented as I sat trembling in his office. "There must be a lot of energy flying around your house. I usually prescribe Prozac for women in menopause. It seems to take the edge off."

Prozac? I wondered. *Why Prozac?*

Even though my sons' doctor did seem confident about his suggestion, to me none of what he was saying was making any sense. Why would I want to take an antidepressant when I didn't feel depressed? I felt anxious, terrified, even wildly crazy, but not at all depressed. Still, since this doctor did seem to know a little bit about how difficult menopause can be for some women, I couldn't help wondering whether he might know anything about some of the other midlife medications I'd been reading about.

"I read something on the internet about some women taking Xanax during menopause," I said. "Do you know anything about that?"

Before I could even finish asking my question, the doctor was already shaking his head.

"You'll want to stay far away from Xanax," he said firmly. "It's way too addictive, especially if you take it too often."

****

With the end of August fast approaching, it was time for me to start getting my sons ready for school, to start buying school supplies and clothing—a task I'd always enjoyed but now, with how little sleep I'd been getting, suddenly seemed impossible. Although there were nights when I was still able to get six or seven hours of sleep, because of how wild and out of control my "disturbances" had become, those nights were becoming fewer and farther between. For the most part, I was only sleeping about two or three hours a night, and some nights, nights when my "disturbances" were especially disturbing, I wasn't able to get any sleep at all. Zero. Zilch. Nada.

It was because of how persistent this sleeplessness had become that although my doctor still wouldn't even discuss bio-identical hormones with me, she did suggest that I try taking another medication, the very same medication my sons' doctor had just warned me to stay far away from.

"Just make sure you only take a quarter of a pill at a time," my doctor advised, "and only when you really need it. Xanax can be addictive if you're not careful."

Yes, yes…addictive, I thought. *So I've heard.*

Even though I had long been opposed to taking any kind of medication unless it was absolutely necessary, especially medication that could be addictive, at this point I was so desperate that I was ready to give the Xanax a try. After all, with everything I'd been reading on the internet, it seemed that, at least for some women, taking Xanax had become a kind of initiatory rite into menopause, a way of christening oneself as an official "menopaus-ee." And, with so many of these "menopaus-ees" seeming to be having so much success with this "medication for menopause," I couldn't help hoping that maybe it would work for me as well. The way I saw it, salvation laid just a short trip to the pharmacy away.

Not so fast, whispered the beast. *Not so fast.*

I'm not sure how many nights I had that bottle of Xanax sitting in my kitchen cabinet before I finally decided to open it, but after three sleepless and "shitty" nights in a row I gave in and took one quarter of a pill as prescribed. Although I did manage to get some sleep that night, the results weren't anywhere near as calming as I'd hoped they would be. In fact, they were downright disturbing.

Journal Entry 8/28/05

> *"…Long about 1:30 I caved and took a Xanax. It did knock me out for about 5 hours but I woke up anxiety ridden and my blood pressure through the roof…Don't think I'll ever take the Xanax again, that's for sure…"*

So, after only one dose of the highly acclaimed Xanax, I vowed that I would never take it again. Ah, but you know what they say about the word "never"…

Like many adult survivors of childhood abuse, I had gotten myself into an abusive marriage, not physically abusive but emotionally and, at times, in ways that felt far too similar to the past that had propelled me there. Since I so needed someone who could help me find a way out of my "disturbances," however, and with no one else to turn to, by the end of August I felt I had no choice but to reach back into my marriage and to my husband for support. Since his career demanded that he spend most of his time on the road, he had missed most of the early struggles of my crisis, but returned on August 30th to spend several days at home. Terrified and desperate, as soon as he came through the door, I began speaking to him again after several months, or perhaps even years of offering little more than the necessary formal pleasantries:

"Did you have a good trip?"
"The car is going to need new tires."
"I want you out of my house."

Things like that.
Having also decided to let my mother back into my life several weeks earlier, I soon discovered that although I was feeling somewhat safer on one level (that at least my sons would have another adult to turn to in case I suddenly keeled over), I was feeling far less safe on so many others. I was feeling so much less safe that a few nights later, sometime around

2 a.m., I decided to toss my vow of "never" overboard and reach back into the kitchen cabinet for another dose of Xanax.

The Perils of Perimenopause

Prozac and Xanax. Who would have thought that these would turn out to be the "medications for menopause"? What kind of feminine disturbance had I fallen into that I would need to take psychotropic medication just to get through it? As I mentioned earlier, I'd always thought going through menopause would be a relatively painless process—one or two hot flashes and, boom, finished. What was all of this talk about antidepressants and anti-anxiety medication? Could going through The Change really be all that bad?

As I struggled to make sense of everything I was discovering about this fascinating and sometimes infuriating feminine process, I couldn't help remembering my experience with one of my earlier feminine processes, one which, because of a similar case of naiveté, also took me a bit off guard—childbirth.

How bad can it be? I can remember thinking just after I became pregnant. *Women have been having babies since the beginning of forever. If it were really all that painful, wouldn't they be a little more hesitant about it? Labor is probably no worse than bad menstrual cramps. It'll be a breeze.*

Ah yes, a breeze.

Mine was a Pitocin labor, the doctor coming in every few hours to turn the drip up, and the nurses coming in after him to turn it back down because they felt so sorry for me. I know. I know. This isn't the most natural birth process, and I'm sure today's more holistically oriented mothers would probably chastise me for letting my doctor talk me into the Pitocin in the first place. Aside from what I'd learned in Lamaze classes about the pros and cons of anesthesia, however, I really didn't know all that much about what my options were during childbirth, and, to be honest, no one ever told me about them either. Come to think about it, other than the anesthesia issue (to which I agreed only to a few shots of Novocain and one of Demerol), I really didn't know I had any options.

All of that aside, even before the doctor started the Pitocin drip, the intensity of my natural labor pains were more than enough to cause me to start rethinking my ideas about labor and menstrual cramps. I can remember walking the halls of the hospital early on in my labor, up one hallway and down another, my hope being to help move the process along a little. As an avid runner, I suppose I had it in my mind that I'd be able to deliver my twins "on the run," so to speak, without even missing a step. That is until a particularly strong labor pain literally dropped me to my knees right there in the hall, and I practically had to crawl back to my room. Several hours later, after four long and grueling hours of pushing on my part and pulling on the part of my obstetrician, pulling and then ultimately yanking, my son, David was born at exactly 10 a.m.! What joy! What excitement! And his brother? Was he born two minutes later? Three minutes? Four? It wasn't until a full hour and twelve minutes had passed that Jonathan finally decided to extract himself from my womb and enter the world—or, more precisely, that the obstetrician was finally able to yank him from my womb and thrust him into the world. Needless to say, it was a rough delivery, something my obstetrician would later jokingly refer to as "the delivery from hell." Had I been naïve about this feminine process, this process of labor and delivery? You betcha! And apparently, fifteen years later, I was still just as naïve about the process of perimenopause.

But how much worse could it get? I wondered as the dog days of August wore on. *This process of delivering my "crone self" into the world…how much longer could it possibly last?*

As my "disturbances" continued to grow more and more challenging that summer, I started asking some of the women I knew about what their experiences with menopause had been like. Actually, I had become so desperate to learn as much as I could about The Change that I even began asking a few women I didn't know, women I'd seen in passing but had never spoken to before. Although some of these women were a bit too embarrassed to talk about their experiences (or maybe it was that they were too put off by my nosiness), others were more than willing to share whatever information they could about the ups and downs of the feminine midlife transition. I can remember speaking to several women who'd had the experience of simply soaring through The Change.

"I didn't even have any hot flashes," one woman told me. "Not really, just a few night sweats, which my husband and I figured we could handle just fine."

Gheez! I thought, my whole body trembling. *Why can't I be more like you?*

But then there were other women I spoke to that summer, women who'd apparently found their transitions into cronehood to be a bit more confounding. I can remember one evening when, out for my usual walk, I ran into a friend of mine. I think she was around sixty years-old at the time, a former dancer with a grace and beauty that continue to compliment her as she ages. She was outside maintaining the gardens at a nearby church when I saw her, surrounded by winsome Lobelia and Alyssum while, entrenched in my "disturbances," I felt as if I were being surrounded by the Four Riders from Hell.

"How long does menopause last?" I asked my friend after we chatted about the challenges of The Change for a few minutes.

"Twenty-one years," came my friend's sure and speedy reply.

Twenty-one years! I thought. *Does that mean I'll still be dealing with my "disturbances" when I'm sixty-seven years-old? I'll never make it!*

Sensing my apprehension, my friend went on to explain. "Twenty-one years," she repeated. "...seven going in, seven during, and seven on the way out."

I'm not sure whether it was a few months later or not until several years had passed, but I can remember, at some point, being able to have a good laugh over those words of feminine wisdom offered to me by my friend. But in that moment, that moment when the Four Riders from Hell were still swirling around me like a swarm of angry bees, I had no idea how I was going to survive the next twenty-one seconds, let alone the next twenty-one years. Up to my eyebrows in the perils of perimenopause, that expanse of time was something I was simply much too terrified to think about.

****

Journal Entry 8/30/05

> "…Guess I'm just not going to be able to get around this
> menopause thing, no matter what I do. There's going to be
> fall out—bad fallout, no matter what…"

It seems apparent that although I might not have wanted
to believe it, at least in some way, I knew. Even in all of
my craziness and in my frantic search to find some "more
curable" explanation for the chaos I was experiencing, some
part of me knew that, ultimately, it had something to do with
perimenopause. It was because of this inner knowing that I
kept finding myself being drawn back to it again and again—
back to perimenopause, back to the feminine cycles, back to
feminine wisdom—back to all of it, for healing, for guidance,
and maybe even for forgiveness. Forgiveness for what, you ask?
Forgiveness for underestimating Her power, of course.

Luckily, it didn't take all that long for me to find the websites
for Power Surge and for "The 34 Menopause Symptoms," both
of which had been extremely helpful in bringing me up to
date on some of the many challenges a woman can encounter
during The Change besides hot flashes. But even with all the
information I was gathering and all the wisdom I was gaining,
I was still spinning, still plummeting deeper and deeper into
some sort of midlife breakdown, a breakdown I couldn't, for the
life of me, understand. I wanted to know more. I needed to
know more, and so, even with all of my confusion and brain fog,
I kept right on searching: the internet, the library, and yes, even
the experiences of the women I'd meet on the street, no matter
how nosy they might have thought me to be.

It was through my hopeful and diligent search that I soon came across a small book in our local library system, a book which instantly became my bible during my crisis—*The Pause, Positive Approaches to Perimenopause and Menopause*, written by Lonnie Barbach, PhD. Even though I first checked Dr. Barbach's book out of the library sometime in late August or early September, because of how reassuring I found it to be, sometimes serving as my only link to sanity, I didn't return it until many months later, in fact, not until sometime the following spring. Fortunately, during the many months that I spent clinging to *The Pause,* no one at the library ever asked about it or charged me late fees. Living in such a small town, even the library director knew I was in a downhill spiral and was willing to make some allowances.

Using my copy of "The 34 Menopause Symptoms" as a bookmark, I referred to *The Pause* often during those early weeks of my crisis, for information as well as for comfort. Given how quickly the intensity of my "disturbances" seemed to be mounting, however, at the time, I don't believe I ever read *The Pause* in its entirety. What I did manage to do was pick out whatever information seemed most vital to me in the moment so that I could then use that information to reassure myself that what I was experiencing was completely normal. One day, terrified by the pounding in my chest, it was the section on heart palpitations I'd turn to. Then, the next day, frantic over the zapping inside my brain, it was the brain static section I'd read. Then, the next day, feeling as if I was adrift on some stormy sea, it was the nausea and dizziness section I'd bury my nose in.

I can hardly believe it, I can remember thinking as I flipped through the pages. *I have this symptom, and this one, and this one, and this one.*

Although everything I was learning about the physical challenges of perimenopause certainly was an enormous comfort to me, it was the information about its emotional challenges that I found to be most reassuring, especially the more severe emotional challenges some women can encounter. In my reading, I was surprised to discover that these more intense emotional experiences are actually much more common during The Change than most people might think. As Dr. Barbach explains, as estrogen levels begin to decrease during perimenopause, fifteen to twenty percent of women will find themselves experiencing periods of *"serious* emotional upheaval," upheaval that, for some, may become so severe that they may even fear that they are losing their minds. Panic attacks, episodes of intense rage, paralyzing anxiety, even psychotic experiences—these are just a few of the more severe emotional challenges described by some of the women in Dr. Barbach's book.

Oh, my God, I thought as I read and then re-read these women's stories. *These women sound just like me! They sound just like me!*

Much like when I first discovered the website for Power Surge and the posts written by the women who were also struggling with episodes of night panic, it was a comfort for me to learn that I was not alone in feeling like I was losing my mind. In fact, each time I was able to find any one of my "disturbances" listed in Dr. Barbach's book, whether physical or emotional, I would begin to feel hopeful that maybe what I was experiencing really was nothing more than an exceptionally difficult perimenopause. The instant I would grab hold of this sliver of hope, however, the instant I would begin to steady myself against it, I'd find myself being swept away by some of the many "disturbances" I was having that didn't seem to be listed in *The Pause* or anywhere—"disturbances" like the "twitch thing" and that God-awful stench, like the electric jolts that would jerk me straight up into a sitting position, and the nights I would spend sitting on the kitchen floor because of them. It was because of these more bizarre "disturbances" and no explanation for what was causing them that even with everything I was learning about the midlife change, I continued to feel more and more panicked over what was happening to me. It was as if there were two forces tearing at me that summer, each feeding off of the other for strength—one, the beast and his barrage of "disturbances," and the other, my panic over these "disturbances" and not knowing what was causing them. As hard as I tried to remain calm and to keep everything in perspective, over and over I discovered that the more frightened I became about my "disturbances," the more intense they would become, these two energies shifting back and forth to create their own out of control mayhem—

"Disturbances" and fear! Fear and "disturbances"!

Back and forth! Back and forth!

As I continued to search the pages of *The Pause* for any information that might offer me even the tiniest bit of comfort, I came across one particular piece of wisdom which, in my rare moments of clarity, I was able to see as being especially significant for my situation. As Dr. Barbach so crucially points out—the more stress a woman is experiencing in her life, the more difficult her transition through menopause is likely to be.

So there it was. Given the stressful circumstances that were surrounding my life at that time—my stressful marriage and the memories of sexual abuse that had begun to emerge—from everything I'd been reading it made sense that my midlife transition was not going to be an easy one, not an easy one at all. The question was, if it was going to continue being as difficult as it had been so far, with my heart's relentless pounding and night after night of little to no sleep, how was I going to get through it?

I can remember at some point that summer becoming so convinced about the hormonal aspect of my crisis that I started having daydreams about bio-identical hormones, daydreams about what it would be like to find a doctor willing to prescribe them for me. In my daydream, I would imagine this doctor giving me a shot of estrogen that, within minutes, would relax me so deeply and so completely that I'd finally be able to fall asleep and stay sleep. And it wouldn't be just for the usual seven or eight hours one would normally sleep in a night, but for twenty or thirty hours, long enough to allow me to finally begin making up for all the sleep I'd been missing. Ah, but that was just a daydream, wasn't it? There was no such doctor, at least none that I could find. So, like it or not, for me, it was going to have to be one of those other "medications for menopause" to come to my rescue. For me, at least for the time being, it was going to have to be Xanax or bust.

SEPTEMBER

With my mind and body still wide-awake and the clock on my nightstand glowing with a bright and mocking 2 a.m., I went ahead and took that second dose of Xanax. Then I went back to bed and waited for the calm to kick in, the ease, the sense of relaxation that would allow me to get the same five hours of sleep I was able to get the first time I took it. But sleep is not what came for me this time. This time, all that came was more of the cursed chaos—more trembling, more heart palpitations, more anxiety, and, with all of it, a far more scathing insomnia.

Oh, my God! Why can't I sleep? I thought frantically. *The Xanax was supposed to help me sleep! What do I do now?*

But no matter how much I moaned and pleaded, no matter how much I begged, I still couldn't fall asleep. For the rest of the night, all I could do was lay there, listening to my heart pound and feeling it crash up against the inside of my chest. I tossed and I turned. I trembled and I shook, and by morning, the first day of September, I was beginning to feel hopeless.

Journal Entry 9/1/05
  *"… I'm truly afraid to try anything at all at this point.
  My darned body is so reactive… It's getting to where I'm
  afraid I won't be able to help myself through all of this. I
  truly don't know where to turn…All I can do at this point is
  keep praying and maybe God will help me…God in heaven,
  I am begging you for help. Begging…"*

So, my hopes that the Xanax would save me had all been
dashed. For some reason, I wasn't like the women I'd read
about on the internet. For some reason, my body would not
be calmed by this "medication for menopause" the way so
many of theirs seemed to have been. Not only that, for me this
seemingly innocent little pill, this benzodiazepine, seemed to
have a whole other effect, one far more frightening than the
racing heart and unrelenting insomnia I was fast becoming used
to. Or was it the marital reconciliation and not the Xanax that
sparked this new "disturbance"?

Although I had barely managed to get even an hour of sleep
that night, later that day I decided to head off to the mall to do
some school shopping with my sons—my husband along with
us. As the four of us began making our way around the store
in search of the usual pens and pencils, subject dividers and
notebooks, something very *un*usual began happening inside my
mind. It was as if I had suddenly fallen through an enormous
crack in some part of my consciousness, a crack that led into
a well of hopelessness and fear inside me so deep and so dark,
I didn't know if I'd ever be able to climb back out. I tried to
keep my attention focused on shopping, looking at the folders
and then at the loose-leaf paper, but nothing I did seemed to

help. No matter what efforts I made to avoid it, there wasn't any way I was going to be able to escape the terrifying reality that some part of me had begun contemplating—no, had begun *threatening* to commit suicide.

Dear God, what's happening to me, I thought, my mind wild with panic. *Why do I suddenly feel like I'm going to kill myself?*

Even with all the confusion and terror that was welling up inside me, I knew it wasn't me who wanted to commit suicide, not the present-day me. I so loved being a mother to my sons, so loved my pets, my writing, and my early morning walks. And yet, something inside of me was in such pain, such deep and wrenching pain.

How to hold on? How to hold on?

Terrified that I might actually try to kill myself, as with so many other things during my crisis, again, I did something I never would have dreamed of doing before—I asked my husband not to leave for his trip the next day. I didn't tell him I was afraid I might commit suicide. How could I admit this even to myself? Instead, I told him I thought I might be losing my mind and needed someone around to help me in case I did.

Although I never expected it, my husband did rearrange his schedule so that he could leave for his trip on Sunday instead of Friday. Again, I was grateful to have another adult in the house in case I suddenly keeled over, or now, perhaps did something even worse. During the two extra days my husband was home, I managed to get a full five hours of sleep one night, and was actually able to get in touch with a pharmacist who said he would work with me on the bio-identical hormones. For a moment, I felt hopeful—shaky, but hopeful.

By the time Sunday rolled around, my husband was packed and ready to leave for his trip. I think this one was for two weeks in Japan.

"You're fine now," he insisted as he hurried out the door. "You'll be fine now. I'll see you in two weeks."

I wasn't fine, not by a long shot, but I had neither the strength of will nor the presence of mind to argue, so without so much as a word from me, my husband was gone. My husband was gone, and, once again, I was left to deal with my "disturbances" alone—alone with my sons watching and worrying from across the divide, from across the chasm that now separated me from the life I knew with them before, a life that included drama camp and plays, music festivals and science projects, and summer nights spent watching shooting stars in a clear, black sky. That was the life I knew before, a life that was now slipping through my fingers like wind through a screen. I had no idea how to find my way back to that life, and no idea where the new life, the life filled with chaos was leading me… where it would lead my sons if I didn't make it out intact… where it would lead them if I didn't make it out alive.

****

It was around this same time, during the frantic days of early September with the intensity of my "disturbances" mounting and thoughts of suicide beginning to dance in and out of my already frantic psyche that I seemed to have reached a crossroads, a moment of reckoning, or maybe it was a moment of simple choice. I was outside walking my dog on yet another late summer evening when I suddenly became aware of some sort of message, a question welling up from somewhere deep inside me. There was no voice with this question, only a firm awareness that it was being asked.

Do you want us to pull you out?

Although I wasn't able to make the connection then, looking back now I can remember that this is a question that had been posed to me once before, on another occasion much earlier in my life and during a much smaller crisis. It was a crisis that occurred while I was competing in a community triathlon in 1985 and during the first leg of the event—the swim.

Truth be told, I was an awful swimmer, always had been, and so, naturally, wound up at the very back of the pack, the back of the pack where I could see someone else who was also struggling—a young man. Like me, this young man was having a hard time keeping his head above the water and so, naturally, reached out to grab hold of whatever was closest to him for support—in this case, me. Since I was having a hard enough time trying to keep my own head above the water let alone both of our heads, I warned the man that I didn't swim all that well, but, with no one else to grab hold of, he continued to hold on to me. Seeing that someone was in trouble, the lifeguards quickly began to steer their lifeboat in our direction and, within minutes, were able to pull the man out of the water. With my enthusiasm for the race only a bit deflated, I wished the man well, took a deep breath, and continued with the swim. I had just about made it to the first turn in the quarter-mile event when, suddenly, there at the back of the pack, I saw another man struggling, struggling and reaching out to none other than yours truly for support. As I had with the first man, again, I confessed that I didn't swim all that well, but, again, with no one else to grab hold of, the second man continued to hold on to me. Noticing this second man's struggle, the lifeguards

immediately paddled back over and began unraveling the
man's arms from around my neck. As they were hoisting him
into the boat, they turned and looked at me as I continued my
enthusiastic and yet inefficient doggie-paddle.

"Do you want us to pull you out?" they asked.

Like that day in the triathlon, when this question was
posed to me some twenty years later during my crisis, again,
I answered with a resounding, "No. No, I want to continue."
Even now, I'm not at all certain whether the question came
to me that evening as the result of some inner prodding, or
if it might actually have come from somewhere or someone
beyond me and my earthly struggle. What I am certain of is
that my reason for choosing to "stay in the race" was so that I
could be here with my sons, so that I could be here to watch
them grow and see what they would do with their lives…to see
what they would become. Although I may not want to admit
it even today, I believe I may also have felt some desire to stay
and see what I would do with my own life, to see what I might
become once I was able to find someone who could help me
with my "disturbances." And so, hands still shaking, heart still
racing, like that day in the triathlon, I took a deep breath and
continued onward.

****

Although I had been lucky enough to find a pharmacist
who said he would work with me on the bio-identical hormone
issue, I still needed to find a doctor who would be willing
to sign the prescription, so on September 6th, the day before
school was to start, I went to see a gynecologist. With only
two hours of sleep and yet another bizarre food reaction (was

it from the bite I took of my son's grilled cheese sandwich or the dash of pepper I'd put on my lettuce?), by the time I got to the gynecologist's office, I was already a shaky mess. As I sat in the waiting room trying to fill out the medical history forms, I could feel those familiar jolts of electricity…waves of terror…of energy…something, welling up inside my chest, welling up and swirling around my body like the tongues of an out of control fire. Worried about how my heart might be reacting to these wild and willful surges, I put my fingertips to my wrist, looked down at my watch, and counted out my pulse for a full fifteen seconds.

…20, 21, 22, 23.

Multiplied by four, that meant my heart rate was ninety-two beats per minute!

I must be dying, I thought as I fumbled with the forms. *Why else would my heart be beating so fast? Oh, my God, I must be dying!*

Once I was inside the examining room, a nurse came in and asked me to roll up my sleeve so that she could take my blood pressure, a procedure that, by this time, also had me out of my mind with fear because of how high those readings had been climbing as well.

"176 over 90," the nurse announced.

176 over 90! I thought. *My blood pressure's never been that high. Never! Something's definitely wrong with me, something bad. I can feel it!*

As I continued to slip deeper and deeper into yet another swell of mind-wrenching panic, the gynecologist came in and looked at my chart.

"So, you're here because you want to go on hormone replacement therapy," she said, taking her seat in a chair across from me.

"Y…yes, bio-identical hormones actually," I replied. "I…I'm having a hard time sleeping. I'm hoping the hormones will help."

The gynecologist reached for a pen. "Yes. Well, it seems that your blood pressure is a bit more of an issue at this point. What is it…176/90? I think we should try to focus on bringing that down and forget about the hormones for the time being."

By the way the gynecologist was looking at me, I could tell that she had already come to the conclusion that I was some kind of "case." Or, maybe it was the way I started asking to be admitted to the hospital psychiatric unit over and over that gave her the clue.

"Just so I can sleep," I begged. "M…m…maybe you can admit me to the psychiatric ward, just so I can sleep."

After reminding me that this particular psych unit was only for elderly patients, elderly patients with serious psychiatric issues and not insomnia, the gynecologist left the room to have a private phone chat with my doctor, who, by the way, was one of her patients. (That's right. This gynecologist was the same one who had warned my doctor that the estrogen she was taking was going to kill her.) After just a few minutes, the gynecologist came back into the room to announce that together, she and my doctor had decided that I should take Inderal, a beta-blocker, for my blood pressure and anxiety. The way they saw it, this was the best medication to help me deal with my condition.

"Oh, and see a therapist," the gynecologist chided from behind her desk as I was leaving. "Then maybe we can talk about hormones."

With little more than a sheepish nod, I turned into the hallway and quietly shut the door behind me. Given how crazy I'd been feeling and now how crazy I was acting, I was beginning to feel rather hideous about myself, hideous and embarrassed—by my blood pressure, by my behavior, everything. But even with my embarrassment, somehow, I still couldn't stop my frightened and obsessive rambling.

"I don't know what I'm going to do," I said to my sons after my appointment, my thoughts racing, my body reeling. "My blood pressure's so high. What's going to happen to me? Am I dying? Do you think I'm going to die? Do you? Do you? Do you?"

I could hardly believe this was me talking and, I'm sure, neither could my sons. Up until that summer, they had always known me to be so steady and sane, the ever-present rock in everyone else's time of crisis. What must I have become to them now that I was so thin, and trembling, and pale? What had I become to myself?

Although I was still reeling from the aftereffects of the Xanax, I was also still so desperate to get more than an hour or so of sleep that after careful and yet frantic consideration, I went home and took a dose of Inderal as directed. I could hardly believe how quickly the medication's tranquilizing effects came over me. After nearly two months of living in a state of rapid-fire frenzy, suddenly I could feel something inside of me being silenced…controlled—not disappearing, mind you, but being controlled. It was as if the Inderal had placed a lid over my confusion and fear, or, better yet, like someone had wrapped a straightjacket around them to keep them contained. Underneath this medication-induced calm, I could still feel every bit of the chaos. I could still feel the beast thrashing, and moaning, and pounding his angry fists up against the inside of my body. It was because of this relentless pounding that, even with the medication, that night, I still couldn't sleep. Instead, I lay in my bed staring at the ceiling, terrified by the power the beast had over me and, even more so, of his persistence.

This can't be good, I thought. *No matter what I do, it doesn't stop. It doesn't stop! All I'm doing by taking the medication is containing the pressure, pushing it down and allowing it to build even more.*

Worried about how holding so much anxiety inside my body might affect me, later that day I started looking up the side effects for Inderal, also known as propranolol, and soon discovered a website with a whole list of them: slow heart rate, congestive heart failure, depression, hallucinations, insomnia. (Seriously?) In my search, I also found a blog for propranolol users where dozens of people were writing about their experiences with some of this medication's more concerning side effects.

Oh, my God! I thought, becoming more and more frightened with each word I read of the posts. *I don't want any of this to happen to me! What am I going to do?*

Only halfway through the blog, I'd already read more than enough. I immediately decided to stop taking the Inderal and to call my doctor, all the while doing my best to work with my body/mind to try to control my rising blood pressure.

155/88.

165/90.

Steady…steady. Breathe…breathe.
135/80.

With my doctor's reassurance that these readings were at least within the normal range, body still trembling, heart still racing, I took yet another deep breath and continued onward—and with me, the now ever-present beast.

****

For the ten years I had been living in my house, I never once had anyone from my family visit me there. It was my sanctuary, a place I had escaped to in 1995 when the effects of my parents' drinking had begun to run all of us aground. At one point, during the summer of 1993, things got so bad and so unmanageable that it soon became obvious that everyone in my family was going to have to be admitted to some sort of psychiatric/rehab facility. Although I was married and living away from my parents at the time, I was there at the house the day the paramedics came to take both of them to the hospital. Although my mother was calm enough to go by ambulance, my father was so angry and so out of control that he had to be taken in handcuffs by police car. It was the second time within eight months that my father had been committed, and, this time, it would take five police officers to get him in a straightjacket. Still, my father's anger could not be contained, his anger or his fear. I know this. I was on the phone with the hospital nurse the night they tried to restrain him and could hear his struggle, his desperate cries for release.

Unlike the rest of my family, alcohol was never something that really appealed to me. In fact, ever since my parents' struggles began to escalate during the 1990's, I've refused to have even a bottle of cooking wine in the house. By the time of my crisis, I hadn't had so much as a glass of wine in well over ten years but even without the ravages of alcohol, now my mind was beginning to unravel. Now I was the one who was frightened. Now I was the one who was desperate—desperate to be released from whatever force had overtaken me, desperate to find my way back to my sons, and desperate to be able to sleep through the night and stop my body from shaking. I was so desperate and so terrified by everything that was happening to me that on the morning of September 11th, I called my mother and asked her to come to my home.

"Don't do it," my sons begged, having witnessed much of the craziness in my family since the mid-1990's. "Don't do it."

In some way, I knew my sons were right. I knew that inviting my mother over was an act that could cause me far more pain than I was already in, but I also knew that someone had to save us. Someone had to save my sons in case I didn't make it, and someone had to save me because I was already so horribly gone. Someone had to be there for all of us, and so, with my mind and my body breaking apart in ways I never could have imagined, I went ahead and destroyed my sanctuary. I could almost hear its bravely forged walls and barriers falling to the ground as I gave my mother a tour of my gardens, my own words of wisdom swirling through my manic and muddled mind—

Be careful what doors you open. You never know what might be lurking on the other side...

About a month or so before my middle-of-the-night panic attack back in July, sensing the first ripples of my crisis, I went to see a social worker. Because of the way her office was set up and the lack of privacy for effective "therapizing," I only saw this social worker for one session, but in that session I told her everything I thought would be necessary to save my sanity. First, I told her about the difficulties in my marriage, difficulties that although I'd never seen them as such, she immediately identified as emotional abuse. Second, I told her about the abuse in my birth family, but more specifically about a particular episode of physical abuse that had begun to come into my mind—a beating I seemed to have suffered when I was just five-years old and which I had managed to lock out of my conscious awareness for over forty years. Actually, to be honest, there were plenty of clues along the way that some sort of beating might have taken place, telltale signs that there was something wrong, something terribly wrong as, not too long after I married my first husband, I began hitting myself in the head. That's right. Anytime I would feel angry or frustrated with myself, I'd start pounding on my head. Over and over I would hit myself, sometimes using my fist and other times a book or cooking spoon, anything I could get my hands on to inflict my angry blows. It wasn't until 1997 when bits and pieces of this alleged beating began to flit into my awareness that I was able to make a connection between my bizarre "coping mechanism" and the event which may have first sparked it, remnants of a beating's fragmented memory arising through the images of another dream...

I'm sitting outside talking to my grandmother. She's telling me about a beating I suffered when I was a child, a severe beating. "You were covered with black and blue marks," my grandmother tells me. "There were black and blue marks all over your body." In the dream, I then go to

my mother and ask her why she did this to me. Her reply?
"Because you were sleeping with my husband."

Looking back, I could remember a day several years before
this dream when my father called my house, hinting at some
awful thing my mother had done and wondering why I couldn't
remember. Could this have been what my father was trying
to tell me—something about this beating? Or had the dream
been a metaphor for some less jarring event, some event less
painful…less mournful? I can't help but wonder now if the real
reason I asked to see my mother that day wasn't so much to
have her help me with my crisis, but to try to uncover whatever
truth there might have been to my dreams.

After a brief tour of my home and gardens and not a word
spoken about my abuse, my mother soon left that afternoon,
but in the backwash of her visit my crisis quickly began picking
up speed—more confusion, more blood pressure spikes, and
even more pounding from the beast. Adding to all of my usual
chaos, I'd also begun to notice a few new physical "disturbances"
beginning to emerge. One was a high-pitched whistling sound,
a hum that, in the middle of the night, I'd often mistake for
tree frogs or crickets. But the nights were cooler now and the
windows often closed.
   What is that infernal noise?
   Around this same time, my electric jolt "disturbances" had
also begun to intensify as on the nights I was able to fall asleep,
I'd often find myself waking up only an hour or two later,
feeling as if my arms were being lifted right off of the mattress,
my teeth gnashing together in an angry snarl.
   Am I having seizures? I'd wonder. *What's happening to me?*

By this time, I was spending most of my waking hours checking my pulse, taking my blood pressure, or frantically searching the internet for some clue as to what might be causing all of this strange bodily chaos. My mind racing with fear, I'd look up the symptoms for one disease and then another and another and another. I was so frantic and so terrified that even while sitting behind the computer, the energy tearing through my mind and body would not allow me to sit still. One moment, I'd feel myself reaching toward the keyboard with my right hand, and, in the next moment, I'd be reaching with my left. I'd sit up in my chair, then back in my chair, and then quickly back up again, all the while searching for a website that could tell me what dreadful disease might be causing this strange and sudden restlessness. In addition to all of these bizarre movements, my mouth had begun to feel strikingly dry—my mouth, my throat, even my eyes…my eyes often so dry that there were times I could hardly blink. It was because of all of this dryness especially as well as the trouble I was having swallowing that, through my many hours of research, I eventually grabbed hold of Sjogren's Syndrome (an autoimmune disease that causes dryness in the body) as the most likely cause for my "disturbances."

That's it! I can remember thinking when I stumbled across the website. *I must have Sjogren's Syndrome. I have all of the symptoms.*

Certainly, I wasn't qualified to make this diagnosis. I was guessing, grasping at straws, but with how out of control and desperate I had become, it seemed I needed something to cling to, some illness to absorb the energy of my mounting fear. Oh, to be honest, at this point, none of that even mattered. For whatever reason, I had decided on Sjogren's Syndrome as my diagnosis, and, as had been the case with so many other things in my life, things like dieting and running, once I had a hold of this diagnosis, it wasn't going to be easy for me to let it go.

****

As I look back on those early months of my crisis, I find it interesting, and perhaps even somewhat amusing, that even in the midst of all of my "disturbances," like the good obsessive-compulsive type I'd always been, I kept taking care of the house—watering the plants, washing the clothes, cooking, and even doing the fall cleaning. Although it would have probably made more sense for me to sit still and finally start taking care of myself, when I think about it now, what else was I to do but keep moving? At the end of the day, after all of my doctor's appointments, my blood tests, and the many hours I'd spend in front of the computer researching, I couldn't just sit there. Because of my efforts to pursue a writing career, except for a few part-time positions I hadn't had a job outside of my home for several years. Now, except for my daily journal entries, I wasn't even writing anymore, so what else was I to do? I couldn't sleep, could hardly eat, and yet I still never felt tired. In fact, I seemed to have more energy than I'd ever had before… nervous energy…frantic energy…and so, logically, needed to direct it somewhere—hence, the frantic researching, hence, the frantic cleaning.

Another interesting thing I noticed amid all of my inner turmoil was that even though I'd been having a hard time driving for years because of panic attacks (to the point where I'd sometimes have to turn the car around and go home), suddenly I was able to drive to all of my doctor's appointments without any such incidents—twenty miles to one doctor, thirty miles to another. Looking back, I'm sure the panic attacks only seemed to have disappeared because of the constant state of panic I was now in, all of my days and nights now stuck together by one enormous and unrelenting panic attack—heart racing, hands shaking, gasping for air and breath. Even if I tried, it would have been impossible for me to discern any one particular episode of panic out of this already panic laden state.

****

Sometime in the late afternoon on September 19th, my husband arrived home after his two-week trip to Japan. Comforted to have another adult in the house again, even if only for a few days, I was able to get six hours of sleep and woke up the next morning feeling surprisingly refreshed, refreshed and even a bit hopeful.

Journal Entry 9/20/05
> *"Oh Lord, I slept. Thank God in the heavens—got like 6 hrs, maybe more. Now if only I could do that every night— maybe I'd get myself back..."*

Having made an appointment to see my chiropractor that afternoon about an old shoulder issue, later that day I got into the car and headed for her office. As usual, the chiropractor twisted my spine and cracked my weary bones, and then spent a few minutes chatting with me about how good the recent rain had been for the gardens. On the way home, I was feeling so optimistic about the sudden shift in my mental state that I decided to stop in a small gift shop to look at the wind chimes and greeting cards, every now and then glancing at my reflection in the front window or in a mirror set up on the earring counter.

I don't look all that bad, do I? I thought, admiring myself in the glass. *Not too bad for a crazy woman anyway.*

Even the drive home that day felt like a renewal of sorts as I gazed out the car window at the babbling brooks lining the road and at the curve of the mountains in the distance.

Maybe I just imagined it all, I thought hopefully. *Maybe I just imagined it all and I'll be fine now. I should probably call my doctor and apologize for all the trouble I've caused.*

By the time I got home, I was so convinced that my "disturbances" were all a thing of the past that I decided to celebrate by eating some peanut butter on a slice of gluten-free bread, a treat I hadn't been able to eat for months but had always been one of my favorite snacks. I could hardly believe how good the peanut butter tasted compared to my usual fare of turnips and broccoli. With each bite, I could feel nearly every cell of my being basking in the sweet, salty flavor when, all of a sudden—

BAM! BAM! BAM!

Within minutes, maybe even seconds, my heart began pounding harder than ever.

BAM! BAM! BAM! BAM!

What have I done? What have I done?

Holding my hand to my chest, I ran outside and began pacing along the fence in my backyard, desperate to keep my sons from discovering what was happening and wondering what I was going to do next. The whole time I was pacing, I could almost hear the beast's frustrated and angry screams.

No! You can't make me eat! I won't eat! I refuse, I tell you! Do you hear me? I refuse!

I couldn't understand what was happening. Was I being punished for some reason, punished for having a few minutes of hope…for eating…for wanting to keep myself healthy and alive? I must have walked along that fence for close to an hour, finally coming back into the house just as the sun was going down, all the while keeping my hand pressed tightly against my chest in a now desperate effort to keep the beast at bay.

****

The next morning, with my husband already rushing around the bedroom, eagerly getting ready for his next trip, I was out in the living room waking up to a whole new "disturbance"—a bone chilling cold. Now, before you go and say something like, "What's wrong with a little cold?" keep in mind that this wasn't the type of cold you'd feel from the air or wind, or even the type of cold you'd feel from a fever. It was a deep, frightful cold that seemed to reach beyond my physical boundaries, beyond them and to the very core of my being.

"I think some sort of cold front must have come through last night," I said to my husband, hoping for reassurance that it was the weather and not my inner chaos causing my sudden chill.

"I didn't notice," he replied matter-of-factly. "It feels about the same as yesterday."

Oh, my God! I thought. *It **is** me!*

Minutes later, with a twist of his key in the ignition, once again, my husband was off, and, once again, I was left to battle my "disturbances" alone. Since I was as terrified by this new "disturbance," this bone-chilling cold, as I had been by all the rest of my bodily chaos, I went ahead and called my doctor—a new doctor this time since, for some reason, mine had transferred all of my records. When the receptionist at the new office answered the phone, I immediately asked if there was any way I could come in to have my thyroid checked, certain that it was some malfunction there causing my sudden cold flash.

"I do have an opening for later this afternoon," the receptionist said. "How's two o'clock?"

"That's fine," I replied, my hopes for a diagnosis climbing. "Yes, yes, two o'clock. I'll be there."

Since I still had a few hours before I would have to leave for my appointment, I decided to go outside to see if I could somehow manage to mow the lawn, my hope being that by involving myself in this normal household chore, I would begin to feel more normal. Unfortunately, that wasn't the case. With every pass I made across the yard with the tractor, I continued to feel worse—colder, more confused, and far more panicked. By the time I got to the last strip of grass, I was so shaky and so cold that I could hardly hold onto the steering wheel. It was just after I decided to put the tractor away that a woman I knew from my sons' school pulled into the driveway. The instant she looked at me, she knew something was wrong.

"I think I should take you to the emergency room," my friend said after I told her my suspicions about my thyroid. "It'll take days to get the results from a test done at the doctor's office. You should go to the emergency room."

The emergency room? That wasn't a place I ordinarily went. In fact, other than the night I went into labor, I couldn't remember ever going to the ER for anything related to my own health issues. Even on that night back in July when I called 911, I don't think I ever planned on actually going to the hospital. I just needed someone to talk to—someone to reassure me that everything would be all right. Still, with how desperate I had become to find out what was causing my "disturbances," I couldn't help thinking that maybe my friend was right, that maybe someone in the ER would be able to help me. So, once again, as with so many other things during my crisis, I did something I never would have dreamed of doing before. I let my friend take me to the emergency room.

****

As best as I can remember, the walls of the hospital were green, a sort of "hospital-green" that reminded me of another hospital from another time and place, only I couldn't remember where or when. The doctor was kind enough—took some blood and, within a half an hour or so, assured me that although my thyroid level had dropped since my last blood test, it was still well within the normal range.

"I'm sure it doesn't have anything at all to do with your cold spell," the doctor said, "or any of your other symptoms."

Much like when I'd seen the gynecologist, I could tell by the look on the doctor's face that he too had already come to the conclusion that I was some kind of "case." In fact, he even mentioned menopause a few times while we were chatting and how often he'd seen women my age coming into the hospital "like this."

After filling out the discharge papers, I pulled myself together as best as I could and slowly made my way back out to the car. I didn't want to have to leave the hospital, not yet anyway. For the first time in weeks, months really, I finally felt safe. Safe meaning that if my heart did suddenly stop or if I did suddenly start choking on something, at least someone would be able to save me. From the very first days of my crisis, it had become nearly impossible for me to feel safe anywhere anymore. All I ever seemed to feel was afraid—afraid of dying, afraid of going crazy, afraid of being afraid. How was I supposed to keep holding everything together when I couldn't even get past my own fear? How was I supposed to keep holding everything together for myself or for my sons?

****

By this time, over two months had passed since that night in July when I called 911, and with each day and each night that hurried by, my "disturbances" continued to grow worse, not only my physical "disturbances" but my emotional "disturbances" as well. I can remember one particularly emotionally disturbing night; I was just about to fall asleep on the living room sofa when, all of a sudden, I felt something inside my brain "switch off." There was an actual "click," a movement of some kind, after which all of my thoughts seemed to go completely wild. Without actually seeing or hearing anything out of the ordinary, I could sense all sorts of bizarre sounds and images swirling around inside me—hideous faces, horrible scenes, each without any obvious connection to each other, to the present time and place, or to me.

"Are you okay?" Jonathan asked as I jumped up off the sofa.

"Yeah, okay," was the only answer I could muster before racing down the hallway and into my room.

As frightened as I was, as terrifying as all the sounds and images inside of me were, I knew I had to get out of there. I knew I had to get out of the living room and as far away as I could from my sons. They had already been through so much, so horribly much trying to deal with all of my physical chaos. I didn't want them to now also have to deal with what, to me, felt like the very last shreds of my sanity beginning to crumble. I felt awful for them, alone in the house with a mad-woman. I felt awful for me.

Once I had managed to make it into my room, I threw myself down on my bed and let the bizarre images inside my mind take over, let them do whatever they wanted with me without making any effort to fight them. My hope, as best as I can remember, was that maybe this was where I'd finally be able to find sleep—not inside yet another losing battle to save my sanity but inside of my surrender to the lunacy. All throughout the night, the images continued to swirl and dance around inside me, merciless and maddening, and all the while dragging me not closer but further and further from sleep.

What's happening to me? I begged. *Please God, what's happening?*

Whatever was happening, it was obviously much worse than I thought, much worse than perimenopause and even worse than Sjogren's Syndrome. With how horribly distorted my mind had become, it seemed obvious that I had to be suffering from some kind of brain disorder, a brain disorder that, after all of my online research, I felt certain had to be the very rare complication of Sjogren's Syndrome I'd read about, a complication known as Cerebral Vasculitis.

Journal Entry 9/23/05

"... while I'd like to chalk it all up to menopause—I am quite certain that I do have Sjogren's. Now this has been going on for years—the dry eyes, the dry mouth, difficulty swallowing....these physical symptoms I can handle but unfortunately, there are cognitive problems with Sjogren's as well due to problems with cranial nerves or blood supply... Needless to say, I'm a little scared. Don't know at all what's

going to happen to me—will I turn into a vegetable in some nursing home like my father? Can't believe things have gotten so bad so quickly for me...The physical stuff I can handle...it's this mental stuff I can't take..."

After even more online research later that day, by the next morning I had managed to convince myself not only that I was suffering from Sjogren's Syndrome and Cerebral Vasculitis, but that both of these conditions were soon going to kill me.

Journal Entry 9/24/05

"Well...it looks like all this praying I've been doing all these years isn't going to save me after all...I'm just so scared, so scared of what's going to happen to me and this life I've built here—my sons, my precious sons and my pets, my house and yard. All so very dear to me and all things I wanted to be here to take care of for decades to come. Guess I won't be living to the ripe old age of 101 like I prayed... I pray that I'll live long enough to hold my grandchildren, to see the boys become men and find their place in the world. I want them to be married, settled and happy and then I'll be ready to check out if I must. So sad. So terribly, terribly sad and here I can't even cry. Think I'm just too scared and too sad...I just love my sons so much, dear Lord and want so much to be here for them. If there are any miracles left there in heaven, please, I could sure use one now..."

Although I'm not at all certain where I got the idea that these two conditions were terminal, I was so convinced that the Sjogren's Syndrome and Cerebral Vasculitis were going to kill me that while talking to my sons' guidance counselor on the phone one afternoon, I decided to tell him the bad news.

"I'm dying," I said calmly as I pressed the phone to my ear. "I think it's from a brain complication of Sjogren's Syndrome, something called Cerebral Vasculitis. I'm worried about how my sons are going to manage after I'm gone."

I then went on to explain to the guidance counselor a little bit about some of my more bizarre "disturbances" and the reasons why I believed they were killing me. Since I'd always been so levelheaded in my dealings with the school, the guidance counselor had no reason not to believe me. After all, along with serving as the treasurer of the PTA and the editor of its newsletter, I'd also worked as the elementary school reading mom and the sixth-grade science class helper. Whatever the field trip, I was always the first parent to volunteer as chaperone, and even developed a newspaper/literary magazine program for the middle school. So, why would this guidance counselor or anyone else think I was crazy enough to be imagining all of this?

In a small town, news travels fast, too fast, and within just a few days one of the teachers from the district was calling my house, kindly offering me the telephone numbers of various specialists she knew of, brain specialists she thought might be able to help me. Although I don't know whether I ever called any of these specialists, I do know that my sons did, all in a desperate attempt to save me.

****

Sometime around 5:30 a.m. on the morning of September 25th I found myself being startled awake by the most intense electric jolt sensation I'd experienced yet, one far more alarming than any of my earlier jolts and that came with a heart rate of just over one-hundred beats per minute. Frantic and disoriented, I leapt out of bed and hurried out to the kitchen to check my blood pressure, discovering that it had reached another all-time high—178/100. Even though it was still early on Sunday morning, I picked up the phone and dialed my doctor's number. Once I was able to get a hold of him and tell him about the electric jolts and the way they were making my muscles tighten and my teeth clench, he said he thought I might be having seizures and advised me to go straight to the ER. Back in the emergency room for the second time that week, I listened nervously, fitfully while the doctor there explained why he believed these middle-of-the-night jolts couldn't possibly be seizures.

"A person doesn't remember when they've had a seizure," the doctor said. "You can't be having seizures if you're able to remember the experience."

I could hardly believe that for the second time that week, I was being sent home from the ER without a diagnosis and, even worse, feeling more frightened than ever. I can remember lying in bed later that night, feeling so terrified and so hopeless that I actually started wringing my hands, wringing my hands and praying out-loud into the darkness, "God, help me! Please help me," having no idea which way to turn or which "disturbance" or remedy to focus on to try and save myself.

Should I stop eating broccoli? I wondered. *Should I stop eating turnips? If I use the progesterone cream, will it make my heart rate slow down or will it make it speed up? Should I stop using it? Should I use more?*

By this time, I was spinning so hard and so fast that it felt as if I had just about reached the center of my whirlwind. Only there was no eye to this foul storm, no calm moment in which I was going to be able to catch my breath. All I could do was keep spinning—worrying and spinning, worrying and spinning. I was so confused that I couldn't even distinguish any one "disturbance" from all the others anymore—"the twitch thing" from the smell, the smell from the racing heart, the racing heart from the madness. Everything had become fused together, all of my "disturbances" now tangled into one large, rumbling mess.

Journal Entry 9/26/05

"Shit—no better. Actually, I had a worse night—only slept an hour, if that, and most of that was spent in those seizure things…God, I'm so scared. I don't want to die and I want my life back—my music, my yoga, my kids, my pets, my house. My sanity. I just want it all back and can't find anyone to help me get there…No way can I believe this is menopause—and if it's my thyroid, how do I take medicine? My body is already racing—what if it speeds me up even more? Damn it! Is there any way to fix this darn thing? I want my life BACK!!!"

****

After yet another night of little more than an hour of sleep, sometime near dawn on September 27th I got out of bed and stumbled into the bathroom. The instant I looked in the mirror, I could see that the glands on the sides of my face, my parotid glands, had become swollen to nearly twice their normal size. Not only that, my skin seemed to have darkened to some sort of sickly yellow. Certain now beyond any doubt that I really was dying, I hurried out to the kitchen and dialed my mother's number.

"I'm dying," I said to her on the phone. "I have Sjogren's Syndrome and I'm dying. I think you'd better come."

Even before seeing how swollen my glands were that morning, I was already so convinced I was dying that sometime around 4 a.m. I started writing farewell letters to my sons, farewell letters in which I tried to tell them everything I would have wanted to tell them during our lives together, but felt I had to hurry with now that I was running out of time.

> "...Carpe Diem," I wrote in one of my letters. "Seize the day. Life, believe me, is much too short not to. We're on this earth but for a moment, the blink of an eye so make the best of the time you're here..."

And these letters of farewell to my sons weren't the only things I wrote while sitting on my bed in those wee hours, all wide-eyed and wide awake. I also wrote something for myself—an obituary, one similar to another I'd read in the newspaper several years earlier.

> "...Grieve for me for a time," I wrote, "then turn your faces toward the sun. That's where you'll find me... Catch you on the other side...God bless you on your journeys and please, remember me well."

With my farewell letters and my obituary finished, as soon as I hung up from talking to my mother, the first thing I did was offer my sons the best explanation I could for what I believed was happening to me—"I'm dying. I think I might be dying"—and then quickly hurried them off to school. Once my mother got to the house, I then spent the rest of the day

anxiously calling various rheumatologists' offices in the hope
that maybe there was still something that could be done to
save me. After listening to my frightened and frantic tale, the
receptionist at one office agreed to have the doctor see me the
next afternoon.

****

The next day, as I was driving my mother and my sons to my
mother's house to collect some of her things, I began to notice
some sort of tingling in my swollen glands, a tingling that some
part of me seemed to suspect was causing them to shrink. In
that instant, somewhere beneath all of my "disturbances" and in
some distant and perhaps still sane part of my psyche, I could
sense a vague awareness that it was *not* Sjogren's Syndrome
that had been making my glands swell after all. That it wasn't
Sjogren's Syndrome or any other physical disease but rather, the
power of my out of control mind, the power of what doctors, at
one time, might even have diagnosed as a case of "Hysteria."

From what I could remember, Hysteria is a once commonly
diagnosed condition believed to cause all sorts of bizarre
physical symptoms in individuals undergoing certain types of
emotional crises, physical symptoms such as blindness, deafness,
paralysis, and in my case—who knows? Maybe even swollen
glands. Although it did seem that I was able to understand this
in some part of my mind (that maybe I was having some sort
of emotional crisis rather than a physical one), with the rest
of my mind already so deeply invested in my self-diagnosis of
Sjogren's Syndrome and Cerebral Vasculitis, the shrinking of
my glands meant nothing to me. As far as my madness and I
were concerned, death was still fast approaching, and if I had

any hope of saving myself, any hope at all, I needed to get to the rheumatologist and I needed to get there fast.

****

With a look on her face that seemed to indicate that like the gynecologist and the doctor in the ER, she too had already come to the conclusion I was some kind of "case," the rheumatologist agreed to run a few blood tests. When she came back into the room with the results, she proceeded to inform me that all of my tests were completely normal, and although my glands were indeed swollen (Aha!), I showed no signs whatsoever of Sjogren's Syndrome or any other autoimmune disease.

"But...but..." I stammered. "What about these spots on my chest, these *petechiae*? Couldn't they be a sign of Cerebral Vasculitis?" (I may have been out of my mind, but I was still a *very* thorough researcher.)

The rheumatologist shook her head, and, if I'm not mistaken, I think I might also have seen her roll her eyes. Either way, it didn't matter. Again, my hopes had been dashed. The one disease I felt so certain would be my "Eureka," my ticket out of this horrible ordeal and to some sort of miracle cure was now a total bust, or at least as far as this doctor was concerned. Even though I was nowhere near as convinced, all that concerned me in the moment was that, Sjogren's or no Sjogren's, I was still a stark-raving mess, unable to focus enough to figure out what my next move should be to try to regain my sanity and my life. I had nothing to hold onto to now, no malady to hurl my frantic energy into in search of salvation. I was lost...lost...and the beast still pummeling from within.

****

Although I had been dealing with heart palpitations throughout the months of my crisis, the night after I saw the rheumatologist my heart began pounding more wildly than ever. As my mother began unpacking her things at my house, all I could do was lay in the middle of my bed, aware of little else other than the frantic flip-flopping inside my chest. There'd be a "thud," an uncomfortably long pause, and then another "thud," and then a "thud, thud, thud, thud, thud, thud....THUD," and then another long moment of me waiting to feel whether or not my heart was going to start beating again.

Am I going to live? Am I going to die?

While the night before, I had been able to curl up next to my mother to get a few hours of sleep, now my frantic heart would not allow for that sort of calm. With everyone else in the house already asleep, my sons in their bedroom and my mother across the hall from them in mine, I continued to wander through the empty rooms, half-angry and half-out-of-my-mind over everything that had been happening to me. The bizarre thoughts and images that had raced through my mind earlier in the month had returned with a vengeance, and since all of this insanity was coming from someplace inside of me rather than outside, there was no way for me to escape it—no place to run away from and no place to run to.

Not knowing what else to do, sometime around midnight I laid down on the floor at the end of the hallway, just outside the bedrooms. Much like that night back in July, as soon as I did, I quickly discovered that I couldn't lay still. Every time I tried, the bizarre images would start bouncing around inside me... swirling, twirling...around and around, not allowing me even a moment of peace. Frightened and frustrated, also like back in July, I stacked as many pillows as I could under my head until my body was more vertical than horizontal, then closed my eyes. After a few minutes, I began to feel myself starting drift and thought that maybe I'd soon be asleep. Instead, I continued this drifting to well beyond where sleep should have caught me, slowly making my way to what felt like the very edges of my being, the edges of where I leave off and the rest of time and space begin.

Relaxing, this leaving…Relaxing, this falling…

I drifted in this half-place for a moment or two, maybe longer, until, all of a sudden, I realized what I was really doing. My mind filling with panic, I realized that I was leaving. Or rather, that my soul was leaving—leaving the confines of my madness and confusion, yes, but also leaving the body that had become my home…leaving my sons! I knew this edge— had been there before during an earlier crisis, only I couldn't remember where or when. In that moment, that moment of terrifying awareness, I knew I had to do something. I knew I had to find my way back to my sons.

What have I done? What have I done?

Wild with fear, I gathered up all the energy I could and started racing back—back across the timelessness of the edge, back across the calm, back across the terrifying stillness, and finally, finally back into the madness and confusion I'd left on the hallway floor only moments ago. The instant before I opened my eyes, I could hear myself crying out, my voice deep and strange and sounding as if I were emerging from underwater.

"Help me! Help me! My heart! Mother, my heart! Help me!"

The instant I heard my voice, I could also hear my sons' voices. They too were crying out, only there were no words with their cries. There were no words, only desperate, guttural bellows uttered in unison.

"Awgh! Awgh! Awgh!"

Screams awash with fear.

Driven by the sound of my sons' voices, I stood up from the hallway floor just in time to see the look on their faces as they came barreling out of their room—wide-eyed and ashen. Not a second later, my mother came running out of the bedroom across the hall, looking even more frightened than my sons.

"It sounded like something from the other side," my mother said, fighting to control her shaking. "Your voice…it sounded like something from the other side."

My sons echoed her from across the hall. "It did, Mom. It sounded like something from the other side."

With no more than a minute or two of hesitation, my mother picked up the phone and dialed 911.

****

"It must have been a panic attack," my mother insisted a few minutes later as the three of us sat waiting for the ambulance. "…just a panic attack. What else could it have been?"

Having had dozens of panic attacks in the past, maybe even hundreds, I knew without question that this was not one. Worried that whatever it was might suddenly happen again, while my mother struggled to find some more worldly explanation for the otherworldly sound of my voice, I sat as motionless as I could on the sofa, doing everything in my power to will my body, to will my *soul*, to stay alive.

Poem written in 2006:

LISTEN

I know that sad leaving of the soul,
late at night,
when everyone else is asleep,
that toppling over the edge chanting,
"I'm out of here!
Let this wrecked life end.
Begin again or not, let this wrecked life end."

I know the relief sweet falling brings.
Finally, a cliff where I can sleep,
psychosis still waiting in the next room,
laughing its full-moon head off.
The curtains are still pulled open,
offering the only place to escape through,
the only place to escape to—
the barren cold night.
Barren.

Listen.
I know that sad leaving of the soul,
late at night.
We're only falling asleep here, you think
until it's almost too late.
Teetering on the brink, you startle, spin around,
and then start racing back,
all the while muttering those same mother sounds—
"Mother, my heart!"

No, I will not abandon this now!
This crawling,
this clawing,
feels like climbing,
fingers and toes dug deep into life's brittle edge,
what little remains whispering,
"Hurry back! Hurry! Before it's too late.
Hurry."

Listen.
I know that sad leaving of the soul
when there seems to be nothing left to do but escape,
all "here and now's" clouded into that awful fate,
like the door in the basement,
unhinged.
All "here and now's" dissolving into "never's"
there on the hallway floor.
"Mother, my heart!"

Listen.
I know that sad leaving of the soul.
Listen.
Listen.

****

Since I live in a very small town, the paramedics were able
to get to my house quickly and were soon in my living room,

taking my vital signs and slipping an oxygen mask over my face. Although they too might have already come to the conclusion that I was some kind of "case," my rising blood pressure and flip-flopping pulse rate were enough to give them pause, pause and reason enough to take me to the hospital.

"Blood pressure—150/100. Pulse—92. Let's go!"

For the full thirty miles that lay between my house and the hospital, I kept a watchful and nervous eye on the heart rate monitor.

...86...88...81...76...

Although ever since the beginning of my crisis, I'd been becoming more and more frightened by how high my heart rate had been rising, after what just happened I was feeling even more frightened by just the thought of my heart rate dropping. I was so frightened that throughout my middle-of-the-night ride to the hospital, anytime I'd see the numbers on the heart monitor begin to fall into the seventies, I'd use my mind to try and force my heart rate back up into the eighties.

...82...76...74...*Oh, no, I'm dying, I'm dying, I'm dying*...87...88...

By the time we reached the hospital, it must have been around 3 a.m. or so. With the monitor still keeping track of my heart rate and me still keeping track of the monitor, the paramedics carried me inside, took care of the necessary paperwork, and were soon on their way. I was alone now, alone in the empty ER with nothing to do but try to make sense of everything that had been happening to me, not just on that night but through all the months of my crisis.

As I lay in my hospital bed, my eyes fixed on the ceiling, I never thought confusion and fear could run so deep. Although I knew I'd had my share of issues with my history of abuse and my panic attacks, I thought that, for the most part, I had my life pretty much together. When the beast first started to rear his frightening head early in the summer, I'd been taking care of my sons and my home, teaching yoga, and finishing up the middle school newspaper. So what went wrong? Over and over, the questions ran through my mind.

What's happening to me? How did I get here? How did things get so bad and how do I fix them?

The instant the ER doctor came over to my bed, I could tell that she, more than anyone, had already come to the conclusion that I was some kind of "case." Unlike the other doctors, however, this doctor seemed angry, annoyed that I was in her ER at all—but because of my insistence that there was something wrong with my brain, and perhaps because she so wanted to get rid of me, she agreed to run a Cat Scan.

Finally, I thought. *A test that will prove that there really is something wrong with my brain, something physical that will explain everything that's been happening to me. Everything.*

"Everything is normal," the doctor announced just a few minutes after the scan was finished. "There's nothing at all wrong with your brain."

There was no way I was going to believe this. I had been trudging through the outskirts of hell far too long to think anything about my brain could still be normal.

"What about an MRI?" I begged. "Please, can you run an MRI? I'm sure something will show up there. Doesn't an MRI show more detail than a Cat Scan?" (Yes, I was still doing my research.)

"You'll have to make an appointment with your own doctor for that," the ER doctor replied. "There's nothing more we can do for you here."

With no physical explanation for either my physical chaos or my emotional frenzy, there was only one route left for me to take. Lost and defeated, for the second time in less than a month, I started asking for help for my mental condition.

"Can you just admit me to the psych ward then?" I pleaded. "Please, I can't go on like this. Can I just go upstairs to the psych ward?"

"There's no one there to admit you," the doctor snipped. "You'll have to go home."

As I made my way out into the waiting room to where my sons and my mother were waiting, I could see that the sun was just beginning to come up over the city skyline. Daylight was coming and here I was with so many pieces from the terrifying night still scattered around me. While morning could have been a comforting sight under very different circumstances, with the look of fear on my sons' faces and still no explanation to offer them for all of my chaos, I felt more out of my mind than ever. And yet, somehow, I also felt more determined than ever to find someone who could give me a diagnosis. If I was going to have to lose my mind, if I was going to have to die, well then, damn it, I wasn't going to do either without first knowing what was causing all of it. Standing in front of a large window watching the city come to life, I took out my cell phone and dialed my doctor's number.

"There's something wrong with my brain," I told the answering service. "There's something wrong with my brain. Please, I need to make an appointment for an MRI."

After listening to my long and tired tale of woe, the woman taking calls for the doctor at 6 a.m. kindly told me that although I'd have to wait and contact the x-ray department once they opened to schedule the MRI, she'd be happy to make an appointment for me to see the doctor in his office later that afternoon.

Given how unsettling the events of the night had been, the drive home from the hospital that morning was an especially difficult one, for me as well as for my sons. It was a school day, after all, and as we drove past the high school I could see that the buses were already lined up out front and beginning to let some of the students off. The school day was starting and here my sons were missing it all, missing it because their mother was losing her mind. Why was all of this happening? Why? I so wished there was something I could do to fix it—for me, for my sons, for all of us. But it seemed that no matter what I did to try and help myself, no matter what route I tried to take in relation to physical illness or to mental illness, I was met only with dead ends and slamming doors. No one could explain what was happening to me, and, even worse, no one seemed to know.

****

I could hear the rain pounding against the car windows later that afternoon as my mother, my sons, and I headed off to my doctor's appointment. I was much too distraught to drive at this point, and too frightened to take my hand away from my chest for fear of what the beast might decide to do next. Once we got to the doctor's office, filling out forms and explaining my "disturbances" seemed like much too difficult a task given my state of mind, and much too senseless a task given the apparent unexplainable nature of my condition. Still, I did my best to check off all the little boxes on the medical forms as accurately as I could, the whole time feeling as if my heart was about to rumble into an exhausted and defeated stop inside my chest.

"It feels like I'm dying," I said to my sons. "It feels like I'm dying right now…right this very minute."

"Hold on," came my sons' anxious and worried reply. "Hold on, Mom. You'll be able to see the doctor in a few minutes."

Once inside the examining room, I curled up into as tight a ball as I could on the examining table and did my best to explain my long list of "disturbances" to the doctor. Every now and then, I'd see him nod his head as he checked my blood pressure and pulse—always elevated now, both of them always high. Although the doctor did insist that my brain was fine and that an MRI would be a waste of time and money, because of my concern over my father's dementia and my fear of it being genetic rather than due to alcoholism, he agreed to write me a prescription for the test. Thinking that my "disturbances" might be due to some sort of endocrine disorder, the doctor thought it would be a good idea if I also had a twenty-four hour urinalysis to check my hormone levels, and then wrote me a second prescription for that. Once my appointment was over, I gathered my things and was about to head out to the car when I looked back to see my mother talking to the doctor just outside his office. At her urging, he then decided to write me one final prescription, this one for Buspar, an anti-anxiety medication.

Because of the frightening experiences I'd had with the Xanax and the Inderal, I refused to even try the Buspar. To be honest, I was tired of having to fight my way out of medication-induced frenzies when I was already having a hard enough time fighting my crisis-induced frenzies. Why add fuel to an already raging fire? As far as I was concerned, it wasn't any sort of anxiety disorder I was suffering from anyway, but a severe case of Cerebral Vasculitis brought on by Sjogren's Syndrome. Hadn't anyone heard me? From what I'd read on the internet, it was this complication of Sjogren's, the Cerebral Vasculitis, that I felt certain would show up on an MRI if I had one. So, the minute I stepped into the house, I tossed the Buspar prescription aside and called the hospital. After listening to my concerns about my father's dementia and his untimely death, the receptionist in the x-ray department agreed to give me an appointment for an MRI the next day, September 30th.

****

Unlike earlier in my search for a diagnosis, I didn't feel any sense of elation over having made the appointment for an MRI. There were no "Eureka's" shouted or even any whispered hopes that I'd soon have an answer for everything that had been happening to me. Actually, I was so far gone at this point that I didn't even believe I'd live to see morning. For the rest of the afternoon and on into the evening, I continued to feel as if I was hovering in between dimensions, in between worlds. Nothing felt sane. Nothing felt solid. Nothing even felt real. I was so convinced I was dying and so tired of fighting death that while lying in my bed later that afternoon, I decided to give up my fight and to try surrendering to death instead.

Is there something a person needs to do in order to die? I wondered as I struggled to release my body. *Is there an act of intention to it? An act of will?*

I could see the numbers on the clock next to my bed changing—

...5:05...5:06...5:07...

…the minutes racing by. How long would it be before I was gone? How long? With my sons standing nervously at my bedside, I was so certain this was the end that although I hadn't been inside a church in years, I started asking for a priest.

"Where's the priest?" I shouted into the air, air that seemed to be growing thinner by the minute in my delusion. "Shouldn't there be a priest? I'm dying, for God's sake. Shouldn't I at least have a priest come and give me my last rites?" I glanced around the room past my sons' startled faces.

"And where's my mother?" I moaned. "Why isn't she here? Doesn't she know I'm dying? Mom! Mom!"

I'm not sure where my mother had disappeared to or why but after a few minutes of my ranting, she came into the room and stood near the wall, solemn and unusually silent. Even in my near "death-state," I couldn't help but remember a few days earlier when I had seen her looking just as solemn. She had come into the living room to where I was sitting on the sofa and sat down next to me.

"I always thought it was all going to catch up with you someday," she said. "I always thought it was going to catch up with you, but not like this…not like this."

All of what was going to catch up with me? I wondered. *All of what? What does my mother know about my life that I don't? What does she know that I still can't remember?*

I looked over at my nightstand and could see the numbers on the clock still changing and couldn't understand why I was still breathing, why I was still alive.

"I want to go for a walk," I announced, sitting up and planting my feet firmly on the floor. "I want to take the dog for a walk in the cemetery one last time before I die."

Shaky from lack of sleep, or maybe from sheer delusion, I climbed out of bed so my sons and I could take the dog to the cemetery. As we stepped outside into the cold, autumn air, I could feel the wind howling and whining around us and see the sky shifting between a threatening gray and a more hopeful blue above. Somewhere underneath this hodgepodge of wind and weather, the four of us started down the road—my sons, my Aussie-mix terrier, and me. It was like so many other walks we'd taken over the years, walks filled with silliness and laughter, only there was no laughter on this walk. There was no laughter, only sadness and fear—sadness and fear for my sons, and madness, nothing but wild and desperate madness for me.

We had only managed to make it a few steps past the cemetery gate when, all of a sudden, I could feel the pounding inside my chest beginning to intensify.

BAM! BAM! BAM!

It seemed as if there wasn't anything I could hear anymore, anything I could feel but that wretched and relentless pounding.

BAM! BAM! BAM!

Oh, make it stop, I begged. *Please, someone make it stop.*

My heart skipped a beat, and then another, and another, until finally, the pounding did stop. The pounding stopped, and, in its place, there was nothing but a confused fluttering. I couldn't breathe, could hardly stand.

Is this it? I wondered. *Is this the end?*

As I struggled to surrender into the spaces in between the fluttering, struggled to surrender to death, I could feel my legs beginning to collapse out from under me, and, in what felt like a sudden gust of wind, my sons' arms folding into mine, catching me before I fell.

"I can't go on," I mumbled, turning back toward the house. "Please. Take me home. I'm dying. I just want to go home."

As soon as we got back to the house, I crawled onto the sofa and began staring out the window at a group of clouds that had gathered on the horizon. Every now and again, I could feel myself slipping away...dozing off, only to be awakened by my sons' startled voices.

"Mom! Mom! Are you okay?"

"Mom!"

I could almost feel myself floating among the clouds now, floating in between the colors of pink and gray that were about to disappear behind the trees. It felt as if I had already died and had become some sort of apparition, a ghost refusing to let go of the earth while, at the same time, racing madly toward the sky.

****

Journal Entry 9/30/05

"...So scared. So scared that I'm dying—and no doctor will hear me...I wish, so wish someone would try to help me. Maybe, just maybe if they did, I'd have more time. I could die, easily die if not for the boys but thinking of them trying to go on without me drives me even more out of my mind than I already am... Got to save me. Got to save me...Let me out of this nightmare. Please. Please. Please..."

As best as I can remember, we all slept in the living room that night—my mother, my sons, and I—all of us still much too frightened by the previous night's episode to try to sleep alone behind closed doors. Somehow, I managed to get three hours of sleep lying there on the living room floor, still waking up every hour or so to check if I was still alive. Much to my surprise and relief, I did wake up the next morning, and, even more surprising, woke up coherent enough to get to my MRI appointment.

The test itself was simple enough. I went to the x-ray department where after assuring me the results would be normal, the technician instructed me to lie down on an examining table, which she then slid into the tube of the large imaging machine. Once inside, I could hear the characteristic clicks and bangs, knocks and thuds. After about a half an hour or so, the technician rolled me back out of the machine and told me the test was over.

"When will I be able to get the results?" I asked anxiously. "When will I know if everything is alright?"

"The neurologist will need to look at the pictures first," the technician replied. "You can try calling your doctor later this afternoon, around 4:30 or so."

Tick-tock. Tick-tock. Tick-tock. Tick, tick, tick, tick, tick, tick!

Waiting for late afternoon was sheer torture. Although I tried to remain comforted by the technician's reassurance that the results of the MRI would be normal, I couldn't stop my racing thoughts.

Could they have actually found something wrong with my brain? Or did the test show nothing at all, like the Cat Scan? Or is there something there...Vasculitis...something that could explain my symptoms...something that might kill me?

I first tried calling my doctor that afternoon around 4:00, but he didn't have the results yet. Then I tried calling at 4:20 and 4:30. Still nothing. Then finally, I'm not sure what time it was, the doctor called me.

"You have some lesions on your brain," he said matter-of-factly.

"Wh…what do you mean?" I asked, the beast already ransacking the inside of my body.

"Let's see, the report here says that there are a few foci of increased T2 signal intensity in the subcortical white matter. We're thinking they're probably from a few mini strokes."

I couldn't understand what the doctor was telling me. Was I going to live? Was I going to die? Did these lesions have anything to do with my "disturbances"?

"What does that mean?" I demanded. "Is there anything I can do? What's causing the lesions?"

"A lot of people have them," the doctor replied. "It really isn't anything to be concerned about although…"

"Although what?"

"Although the neurologist did say you're rather young to have them. They are rather unusual in someone your age."

I don't know whether it was immediately after talking to the doctor that afternoon, or if it was the next day, or even sometime the following week, but, at some point, I can remember standing in front of my house and slowly sinking down along the clapboard until I was sitting on the ground. I could hear myself screaming although I'm not sure whether or not I actually was. I do know that I was holding my head in my hands, begging someone to help me as I could feel some enormous, black curtain beginning to descend over my mind. I could feel it, sense it…so large and tangible. Nothing but an enormous blackness. It was as if everything inside of me was shutting down, shutting down and dissolving into this hideous blackness—my thoughts, my passions, my dreams—all of these essences of my being suddenly being ripped away from me and hidden behind this heavy, black weight. And, as with all of my other "disturbances," there was nothing...nothing I could do to stop it.

Mental Illness or Menopause

Ever since I first started remembering my childhood abuse in 1993, I knew that I was going to need to work on healing from its aftereffects. I knew I was going to need to do this, and vowed that, someday, I would get around to it. Having my suspicions that this healing might prove to be a bit challenging, a bit overwhelming, I decided early on that this "someday" was going to have to wait until after my sons got out of high school. As far as I could see, this was the only timeframe that would give me the time and space I needed to unravel the events of my past, and my sons the time and space they would need to steer clear of the debris from the unraveling. Not once did I ever consider the possibility that some power beyond me and this well-fashioned plan might intercede just as my sons were entering high school and demand that I start unraveling then. I always thought I'd have some choice in the matter, some choice as to the when and where, and perhaps even the how of the unraveling. Actually, come to think about it, when I look back over some of my earlier emotional crises, I believe there were times when I might actually have had this choice, times when

I would feel the beast beginning to rumble up and was able to coax him back into his cage.

Down, you monster! Back into your cage!

I can remember one of these earlier beastly rumblings occurring just as I was about to graduate from high school. It was near the tail end of my more intense anorexic days when I was around seventeen years-old that I began to feel as if I were, well, melting—some energy inside of me starting to give way and the rest of me struggling oh, so hard to keep it contained. Much like during my perimenopausal crisis, in addition to my struggles with sleeplessness and food, this high school crisis brought with it some unusually obsessive concerns about my body, one of the more persistent of these obsessions centering on a gnawing pain in the pit of my stomach, right smack in the middle of my solar plexus. As soon as the pain hit, I instantly began thinking I had stomach cancer.

Oh, my God! I must have stomach cancer. What else could it be?

Back then, just a budding researcher, I started spending much of my free time sitting on my bedroom floor with a copy of *The Merck Manual*, a medical reference book open in my lap. Over and over, I'd flip through the heavy manual's pages, desperate to find some other illness or condition besides cancer that might be causing my stomach pain. (Is it me or is this beginning to sound agonizingly familiar?)

And what about this bump on my arm? I can remember wondering as I ran my fingers along a gentle rise on the side of my forearm. *Is this cancer too?*

Already frantic over the pain in my stomach, I became so worried about this innocuous bump that I began asking other people what they thought it might be.

"Is this cancer?" I'd ask my boyfriend's mother, a licensed
EMT. "Do you think this bump on my arm could be cancer?"

After a few weeks of this frantic wondering and worrying, I
came down with the flu and tried to convince myself that it was
the prescription cough medicine that had been making me feel
and act so strangely—making me feel as if I had been running
through some dark forest without the benefit of my skin. But
even after I stopped taking the cough medicine, the pain in my
stomach continued—the pain in my stomach, the bump on
my arm, and, with these ailments, the obsessive wondering and
worrying.

It was around this same time, or maybe a little earlier, that
I began seeing a gynecologist about the problems I was having
with amenorrhea—the stopping of my menstrual cycles due
to my anorexia-related weight loss. As I lay there on the
examining table, my pants nowhere in sight and my feet braced
in the icy-cold stirrups, the gynecologist made a rather startling
comment—

"I've been looking at women's bodies for nearly thirty years.
You look disgusting. You're nothing but a bag of bones."

Ouch!

I'm not sure whether it was from that rather unprofessional
comment made by my doctor, or whether it was from having
reached my own crossroads in my myriad of mind/body
disorders, but not long after that exam I noticed the energy of
my anorexia beginning to shift. Instead of being able to remain
loyal to my well-controlled process of self-imposed starvation, I
suddenly found myself being swept away by these wildly out of
control episodes of binge eating. No matter how hard I tried,
I was no longer able to maintain my meager but safe daily diet
of a few stalks of broccoli, an egg white or two, and maybe a

dab of mustard. Instead, I began stuffing myself with all sorts
of foods, odd combinations and gross amounts of foods that,
just a few weeks earlier, I never would have dreamed of eating.
I can remember sandwiches made from gobs of butter and
handfuls of peanuts that I would eat until my stomach hurt;
conglomerations of shortening, sugar, and flour that I would
mix and never get around to baking; and, in between all of
these more bizarre concoctions, entire half-gallons of ice cream
that I would shovel into my mouth until they were nearly
gone. It's not that I chose to eat this way. Quite the contrary;
I desperately wanted to be able to keep starving myself and
to keep losing weight, but there was something inside of me,
something driving the eating—some unseen beastly force.

Disgusted by myself and by the amount of food I was eating,
I did try to make myself vomit once or twice after these binges
although, fortunately, this type of purging didn't work for me.
No matter what dreadful technique I'd use to try to get the
food out of my stomach, my body kept insisting on keeping
it inside. Desperate to rid myself of the food, but even more
so of the shame that always seemed to come along with it, I
soon reverted to episodes of fasting as a way of offsetting the
binging. Binge and purge. Starve and stuff. Such a damnable
cycle, and, as I mentioned earlier, I had gotten myself caught in
this web of disordered eating long before most people had even
heard of these self-destructive coping mechanisms—anorexia
and bulimia. Certainly, long before I'd heard of them. Terrified
by how this beastly force of binging and starving was beginning
to take over my life, I realized that if I was ever going to get
past it, I was going to need some help.

Although I never mentioned my issues with binging and
starving to any of my friends, at some point a friend of mine

told me about the difficult time she was having trying to
control her marijuana habit, about how after smoking pot a
few times with her boyfriend, she found herself obsessed with
it and unable to stop. Not knowing what else to do and too
embarrassed to face her parents, this friend decided to write
her mother a letter explaining what had happened and asking
for her help. As soon as my friend's mother read the letter, she
took my friend to see a therapist where she was able to get the
help she needed to distance herself from the boyfriend and
from the marijuana. It was because of how similar my struggle
with food seemed to be to my friend's marijuana habit that
after devouring nearly an entire tray of cookies one hot summer
night, around two dozen or so, I decided to write my own letter.

"*There's something wrong with me*," I believe is how I began.
"*I can't stop eating. I ate almost the whole tray of cookies that were
in the refrigerator. If you don't believe me, go in and look. I think I
need help.*"

Once I finished writing, I crept into my parents' bedroom
and carefully slipped my letter into my mother's jewelry box.
Then, I went back into my own room and waited. I waited
for my mother to find the letter so that she could get me the
help I needed, the help that would finally enable me to get
control of my eating and my life. Days passed, then weeks, and
soon several months and still no help came. Had my mother
ever found the letter? Had she read it? Or had it somehow
managed to get thrown in the trash by mistake? By this time, I
was far too ashamed to ask my mother about the letter, or to try
speaking to her face to face about my struggles. Instead, I did
my best to bury the incident as far back in my mind as I could,
and to move forward as best as I could, all the while with the
beast still nipping at my heels.

In my effort to try to understand my struggles with food, once I started college I decided to take a course in nutrition. One morning, in between explaining the difference between fat-soluble and water-soluble vitamins, the professor started telling the class about the new hobby he'd taken up—running. From the way the professor explained it, although the reason he started running was simply to lose some of the weight he needed to lose, he soon discovered that this new hobby had a few other benefits as well.

"By the time I get home from a run I don't feel angry or upset anymore," the professor said excitedly. "I feel on top of the world, so much more sane and stable."

It was because of this amazingly positive emotional effect reported by my professor that I decided to start running that very day. I could hardly believe when, within just a few weeks, I too was beginning to feel more sane and stable and, even more surprising, much less inclined to starve or binge. Instead of being obsessed with food and weight most of the time, with calories and grams of fat, suddenly I was obsessed with mileage and running times instead. Granted, I was still just as obsessed as ever, but at least it wasn't with starving and binging.

A few months after I started running, still the budding researcher, I stumbled across a book titled, *The Joy of Running*, written by psychiatrist, Thaddeus Kostrubala. In this book, I discovered how Dr. Kostrubala had actually begun to use running as a form of treatment for a young woman suffering from anorexia. From what I understand, it's the positive effect that exercise can have on a person's mood combined with the way it's able to provide some anorexics with a healthier way of controlling what's happening to their bodies that made running

such a viable treatment. I have to admit, I felt pretty proud of
myself after reading Dr. Kostrubala's book, having been able
to discover this "quick fix" for my food issues all on my own.
Although at the time, I still had no idea what might have
driven me into that dreadful pattern of starving and binging, I
was grateful that my running hobby…my running schedule…
okay, my running *addiction* was enough to get the beast back
into his cage, at least for the time being.

Although there were many scuffles with the beast over
the years that followed, and even some rather intense battles,
it wasn't until just after my sons turned eight and I was in
my late thirties that I was confronted with an all-out beastly
attack. Having begun to have more and more dreams about
my childhood abuse since those first dreams in 1993 and 1997,
early in 1998 I decided it might be a good idea if I went to see
a therapist, my hope being to get a jump on the more intense
therapy I was planning for after my sons graduated. After
explaining a little bit about my abuse to one therapist on the
phone, she thought she might be able to help me, so we set up a
schedule of regular weekly sessions.

As is common with many survivors of childhood sexual
abuse, maintaining a healthy adult sexual relationship isn't often
easy. When one considers how most sexual abuse survivors
have been introduced to sex through manipulative and even
violent means, certainly this makes sense. As many researchers,
authors, and clinicians in the field have pointed out, even once
the survivor reaches adulthood these early abusive experiences
will often linger deep within the psyche, causing the survivor
to view sexuality not as a gateway to intimacy and pleasure, but
as an arena for betrayal, shame, and fear. It was this aftereffect

from the sexual abuse of my past combined with the emotional abuse I was experiencing in the present that was making sex nearly impossible for me—an issue that quickly became a hot topic in my marriage as well as in my therapy. During one of my more difficult sex-related therapy sessions, as I was explaining some of the reasons behind my struggles with intimacy to my therapist, she offered me some rather startling advice—

"You'd better start having sex with your husband or get out of your marriage."

Although I barely even acknowledged this morsel of guidance during my session, once I left the therapist's office it became obvious that it had made far more of an impression on me than I realized.

As I was driving along a rain-swept road later that morning, I felt something inside of me shut down…slip out of consciousness. To be honest, I'm not sure what happened. All I know is one minute I was driving, and the next minute I was being startled "awake" by the sound of a truck horn blaring behind me.

Beep, beep! Beep, beep!

It wasn't until I heard the horn that I was able to come to my senses enough to realize what was happening. For some reason, I had stopped my car in the middle of the road and was now frantically pushing down on the dashboard—literally pushing with my hands—in what seemed to be a desperate struggle to keep whatever was stirring inside of me from rising to the surface. The whole time I was pushing, I could feel this God-awful rumbling. I could actually feel it and hear it, adding even more confusion to my already chaotic state. As I continued to slam my hands against the cheap plastic dash, over

and over my thoughts kept grasping at this one vital truth—
that at 3:30 that afternoon my sons were going to be waiting
for me to pick them up at school. My sons were going to be
waiting for me with their backpacks and homework and with
their Power Rangers lunch boxes, and, no matter what it took,
I was going to be there for them. No matter how hard I had to
push on that blasted dashboard and no matter how hard I had
to fight to rearrange my damned "inner energies," I was going
to be there for my sons.

"Oh, dear God, not now," I could hear myself begging each
time my hands met the dashboard. "Please God, not now!"

It wasn't all that long before this middle-of-the-road
episode that I'd already begun to suspect that there were
some rather unusual things going on inside of me, things
that seemed to indicate that I had these separate parts to my
personality, distinct identities, each with different thoughts,
different wants and needs, and even different memories about
my life. Although my earliest glimmer of this fragmented-
self may have come years earlier when I first began to realize
I couldn't remember anything about first grade, it was during
an argument with my father in 1993 that this theory began to
grow more believable, more urgent...

I was in my parent's basement on a late autumn afternoon,
arguing with my father about his drinking. He hadn't even
been out of the psychiatric hospital a week and already he was
making his way through bottles of gin as if they were water. In
what seemed to be an attempt to even the playing field during
our argument, my father made some comment about the man I
was "sleeping with," a man who was twenty-two years my senior

and who would later become my second husband, my husband
during my perimenopausal crisis. Although I don't remember
exactly what my father said to me that afternoon, something
about my sex life, I'll never forget what I said to him in reply—
   "Well, I'm not supposed to be sleeping with you!"
   The day I hurled those words out across my parents'
basement, the thought that my father might have molested me
hadn't even crossed my mind. In fact, it wasn't until several
months later that the dreams about my abuse began to surface
so, naturally, the words I'd spoken took me off-guard. And yet,
I still couldn't help but wonder, was this true? Had I, at some
point, been "sleeping with" my father?
   Not knowing what to do, I looked at my father, hoping he'd
be as shocked as I was and that he'd say something to make
it not true, to make it all go away, but he never said a word.
Instead, he just stood there staring at me, all the while jingling
the few pieces of change in his pockets with his hands. As I
was struggling to figure out what to say next, all of a sudden, I
could hear someone applauding at the top of the stairs.
   What the...?
   It was my mother. Although I can't be certain, it seemed
that she had been sitting there listening to my father and I
argue and had heard every word he and I said, every word, each
one of those words seeming to hold some bit of truth about my
past.

   Once this argument was over, I quickly put my suspicions
about my fragmented-self and my alleged abuse on the back
burner as I continued to try to deal with the fallout from my
family's drinking while, at the same time, taking care of my sons
and juggling the legal issues of my divorce. It wasn't until I

decided to marry my second husband several years later in 1997 that the most convincing argument about my fragmented-self would come barreling out of my psyche...

Having decided to make my wedding dress rather than buy one, I sat down behind my sewing machine one afternoon and was about to baste a panel of lace onto the silk fabric when, from somewhere in the very back corners of my mind, the strangest thought arose—

I wonder what **she's** *going to do when* **she** *comes back and sees that* **we're** *married.*

She? We? Although I had suspected for some time that this game of hide and seek had been going on, it wasn't until that thought emerged that I was able to realize there really was this other person inside me, this "other" who, from what I could gather, was not going to be at all happy about my upcoming nuptials. And, if there were two of these "others"—one who wanted to get married and one who didn't even seem to know about the wedding—I had to ask myself, could there be more?

It was because of my suspicions about these "others" and my curiosity about how they functioned that once I was able to pull myself together that day in the middle of the road, I decided to keep driving to my destination—a sewing machine repair shop in a town across a nearby river. As I struggled to keep my car steady on the bridge, I couldn't help wondering what was going to happen once I reached the shop. Would I still feel the rumbling, the rumbling and the desperate need to keep pushing whatever was causing it back down? Or would one of my "others" appear, an "other" who was safe from the rumbling?

I have no idea how I was able to keep driving that morning, but, before long, I found myself pulling up in front of the repair shop. I could hardly believe that even as I was stepping out of the car, the bottom of my shoe hitting the rock-hard pavement, I could still feel the rumbling. It was as if there had been an earthquake that only I could hear, a tremor that only I could feel. Then, even as I was stepping up onto the first step of the building, and the second step, and the third…still that awful rumbling.

Is it ever going to stop?

It wasn't until the moment, the very moment I stepped through the door of the shop that, all of a sudden—

"Hi. I'm looking for a new foot for my sewing machine."

It was as if a different person walked through the door—bright-eyed, friendly, and upbeat. Certainly, this wasn't the same woman who, only minutes ago, was sitting in the middle of the road, slamming her hands against the dashboard. That woman was clearly falling apart. This woman, this woman in the repair shop, well, she was obviously much more together. This woman was sane. This woman was stable.

****

Little by little, over the next few years, these "others" began making themselves known to me. There was the "other" who wanted to be with my husband and the "other" who hated him, the "other" who wanted to keep everything together and the "other" who wanted to tear it all apart. But most especially, there was the "other" or "others" who were releasing my memories of abuse to me through dreams in the dark, fretful nights.

Wanting to find out more about these "others" and how living with them might affect my sanity and my quality of life, at some point back in 1998 I began searching the internet to see what I could find out. I believe it was from having seen the movie *Sybil* several years earlier that I decided to use the words "Multiple Personality Disorder" for my search. Within just a few minutes, this search led me to the website for *The Sidran Traumatic Stress Institute* or *Sidran,* an organization whose mission is to help people understand and manage the aftereffects of trauma as well as issues related to Multiple Personality Disorder, or what is more widely known today as Dissociative Identity Disorder (DID).

It was while reading the many pages of information available on the *Sidran* website that I learned that dissociative disorders are not as rare as many people might think. In fact, they're a rather common aftereffect of having experienced severe trauma in early childhood, the most common types of trauma to lead to dissociation being repeated physical, sexual, and/or emotional abuse. I also learned that there are varying degrees of dissociation ranging from the simple daydreaming most of us do every day, all the way to having distinctly separate "identities," identities that are often referred to by mental health professionals as "alters." From what I understand, the abused child is able to create these alters primarily through the power of her/his imagination, by imagining her/himself to be somewhere else or someone else while the abuse is occurring. Should the abuse continue in the long term, these identities or alters become locked in the child's psyche as distinct aspects of her/his personality. Depending on the level of abuse and on the child's stress, the child may soon begin "switching" between these alters or identities not only during episodes of abuse but any time s/he feels frightened or anxious, even during something as non-threatening as giving a report in school or going to a dance or other social event. Over time, these alters will each develop their own way of perceiving themselves and their environment, not only in the present moment but also in how past events were experienced. As a result, some alters will remember the episodes of abuse while other alters along with the "core personality" may not. This type of trauma-related forgetting is a condition often discussed in mental health literature as "dissociative amnesia." In addition to amnesia, some of the other symptoms of dissociation may include insomnia, panic attacks, psychotic-like symptoms, eating disorders, and even self-inflicted or other types of violence.

While dissociation can be an extremely valuable survival tool for the abused child, helping her/him to survive what might otherwise be a life of unbearable abuse, once the child reaches adulthood the pattern of dissociating or "switching" can become extremely disruptive to adult relationships and responsibilities. Often just as disruptive are the post-traumatic stress symptoms that often accompany dissociative conditions, symptoms that, like dissociation, may include insomnia, panic attacks, anxiety, and even flashbacks to the traumatic events.

Although both of these rather common aftereffects of childhood abuse—dissociation and post-traumatic stress—are generally considered by professional mental health clinicians and laypeople alike to be forms of mental illness, even with all of the symptoms of these conditions I seemed to be exhibiting, I never thought of myself as being "mentally ill." After all, despite my issues with food and weight, with panic, anxiety, and insomnia, I'd been able to live a full and active life, earning both my AS and BS degrees with honors, and then going on to have not one but two challenging careers, one as a lab technician and another as an accountant. I'd had numerous friends and romantic relationships over the years and felt blessed to have become a happy and busy mother of twin sons. Certainly these weren't the experiences of someone who was suffering from some sort of mental illness, were they?

It wasn't until the "disturbances" of my perimenopausal crisis hit full force that summer that, looking back on the incident in the middle of the road as well as on my high school crisis, I realized I had no choice but to start rethinking the status of my mental health. After all, by then my struggles with insomnia, panic, and anxiety were reaching an all-time high, leaving me sleepless and frantic nearly twenty-four hours a day. Not only that, although I wasn't hearing voices or seeing things that weren't there, I was definitely smelling something that wasn't there, a hallucination that, by late September, had me thinking not only that I might be mentally ill, but that I was most probably suffering from one very specific form of mental illness—schizophrenia.

Could this be some sort of schizophrenic hallucination? I began to wonder. *Could this awful smell I keep smelling be a symptom of schizophrenia?*

Although I had always believed schizophrenia to be an illness that manifests solely during young adulthood, something I should have been safe from by the time I reached my late-forties, I couldn't help remembering an aunt of mine who had been diagnosed with mental illness sometime during her late-forties. Was that illness schizophrenia? I couldn't remember. Unable to get this aunt or her illness out of my mind, in addition to searching the internet for information about Sjogren's Syndrome and Cerebral Vasculitis, I soon began looking for information about schizophrenia as well, about what types of symptoms it involved and at what age it was usually diagnosed. One morning, as I was scrolling through the information on the website for *Athealth.com*, I could feel nearly all the blood drain from my face when I discovered some rather startling information. According to recent studies, "…for some women, schizophrenia does not develop until after menopause. This delay is thought to be related to the protective effects of estrogen, the levels of which diminish at menopause."

As I continued reading, I found myself becoming more and more panicked as I began to discover what some of the other symptoms of schizophrenia were besides hallucinations, symptoms I felt certain I had. For instance, even though I felt absolutely terrified by everything that was happening to me, I wasn't able to cry, not a single tear, and saw this as "affective flattening." Then, there were the unusual jerky movements I kept making while sitting behind the computer, something I saw as a perfect match for the "unusual motor behavior" symptom described. What seemed to be the most convincing, however, was the obsessive worrying I'd been doing about what was going on inside my body, a symptom of schizophrenia described on the website as "somatic preoccupation."

Oh, my God, I thought. *I really do have schizophrenia! I have all the symptoms! What am I going to do now? What am I going to do?*

By this time, the beginning of October, I was becoming more and more convinced that the reason behind all of my emotional "disturbances" had to be some sort of schizophrenia, a schizophrenia brought on by the hormonal changes of menopause, by my childhood abuse, or maybe even by the

Cerebral Vasculitis of my ever-worsening Sjogren's Syndrome.
Whatever the cause, the only way I could see of being able
to rescue myself from this madness as well as from my fast-
approaching death was to continue to devote all of my time and
energy to my search for a doctor, a legitimate diagnosis, and a
cure.

OCTOBER

Even though I had just been to the hospital the day before for my MRI, by the evening of October 1ˢᵗ I was already frantically rushing back to the ER. Only this time, it wasn't the usual brain disorder I was panicking over but something in my chest, some sort of cough or dryness, a "disturbance" that, to me, meant I had to be suffering from a severe case of pneumonia. And it wasn't just any pneumonia I was worried about, but a very specific type of pneumonia, a type of pneumonia that, through my many hours of research, I knew to be another rare complication of Sjogren's Syndrome.

See, I really do have Sjogren's, I told myself. *It's in my brain and in my lungs. I really do have it.*

As I sat in the ER waiting room with my mother, again and again, I could feel a deep, rumbling cough rising up from inside my chest, and, again and again, I struggled to clear it, certain that if I wasn't able to find a doctor who could help me right away, I'd soon be dead. By this time, it seemed that all the doctors and nurses in the local ER had that look on their faces that meant they too had come to the conclusion I was some kind of "case." Or maybe it was because they had heard all about me from some of the other doctors that they had this notion. Or maybe it was because, by this time, I truly was a "case."

After listening to me prattle on about my "disturbances" for a few minutes, and about my fear of advanced Sjogren's Syndrome and Cerebral Vasculitis, one of the ER doctors very kindly and patiently, and perhaps even a bit patronizingly, agreed to run a few tests on my lungs. For the second time in two days, my body was rolled into some kind of large machine that clunked, sputtered, and whirred, and then spat me back out into my self-spun terror. The results? Everything clear: my lungs, my bronchioles, everything—except, of course, for my blood pressure and pulse, both of which were, as usual, elevated.

"What you need," one of the ER nurses announced, "is anti-anxiety meds. I've been taking them for years and I feel great!"

Well, bravo for you, I thought snidely. *Bravo for you and your prescription drug habit.*

Figuring things would go a whole lot better for me if I minded my manners, already knowing the answer I looked at the nurse and, instead of hurling insults at her, very politely asked, "Do I look like I'm nervous to you?" Both the nurse and the ER doctor stared at me.

"No, actually you don't," the nurse replied. "It's really strange given how high your pulse and blood pressure are, but you do seem rather calm."

This was something that seemed to be making it rather difficult for the people around me to take me seriously, especially medical personnel; I usually remained so unnervingly calm on the outside. Even though I felt clear out of my mind and wanted to scream and tear my hair out, each time I

went to the ER or to a doctor's appointment I would explain
my "disturbances" as if I were describing something out of
a textbook or internet article—all sterile and removed. It
was because of this outward display of calm that, despite my
elevated pulse and blood pressure, the doctor decided against
anti-anxiety meds, and, because of my persistent insomnia,
instead wrote me a prescription for Ambien, a sleep aid.

   "Once you're able to sleep you'll be fine," the doctor insisted.
"You'll feel a hundred percent better."

   Knowing how addictive sleep aids can be and still reeling
from my experience with the Xanax and the Inderal, I was more
than a little leery about taking the Ambien. Since I was also
still desperate to get more than an hour or so of sleep, however,
I decided to take one quarter of a pill that night like the ER
nurse suggested. Glory hallelujah! I was able to sleep. In fact,
I was able to get a whole seven hours of sleep, and, by morning,
was so thrilled with the Ambien that I began considering a
more medication-based approach to all of my ills.

   Journal Entry 10/2/05
       *"... Think I better try Lunesta—less addictive. Do I need
       antidepressants? Anti-anxiety meds? Do I need medicine
       for the lesions in my brain? Want to be Mom to my kids
       again and I'll do whatever it takes—whatever it takes to
       accomplish this..."*

   Having been able to get a full seven hours of sleep with the
Ambien that first night, I decided to try it again the following
night. This time, however, I was able to get only about five
hours of sleep and woke up the next morning wallowing in a
whole new "disturbance." It was as if, overnight, I had been

transported to some blurry Land of Oz or to the other side of someone's looking glass, everything around me suddenly cast in a strange and eerie glow. I was dizzy, confused, and, much to my horror, spiraling into an even deeper despair.

Journal Entry 10/3/05

"So much pain, so much fear, anger and pain. Who can help me out of this? Help my sons? I've been searching and searching the internet for help—but what I find does not sound good—not when this blasted thing is in your brain. Why couldn't I have had some other symptom that might have alerted some doctor to something? Now, I fear, it is most likely too late. Needless to say, I can't sleep, can hardly eat. I'm out of my mind with worry about my sons..."

Since I had just finished the twenty-four hour urinalysis suggested by my doctor and was hoping the results might offer some clue to a diagnosis, once I managed to get David and Jonathan off to school, I grabbed my jug of pee, hurried my dog into the car, and started for the hospital. I hadn't gotten even a mile down the road when, all of a sudden, I began to notice a thick, heavy fog rolling off of the nearby hills and out across the road, the kind of fog that, even for the clearest of minds, makes it damn hard to see. Given my medicated murkiness, being able to see wasn't the only thing I was having a hard time with. Keeping my mind focused on driving was nearly impossible.

Look at all of this mist, I marveled as I gazed out the windows and into the hills. *It all looks so magical, so mysterious.*

Needless to say, a fog-covered country road is no place for a medicated mad-woman to be sitting behind the wheel of a car. There was far too much to distract me, not only with my inner fog but with the fog outside now as well. Fortunately, by the grace of some power much higher and saner than me, I was able to make it to the hospital safely. Once there, I handed my jug of pee over to one of the technicians and then hurried off to make an appointment for the next test on my list—an EEG that would record my brain wave function and which I was able to schedule for the very next day.

****

Because of the peculiar way the Ambien had affected me that morning, in all likelihood endangering my life and everyone else's on that fog-covered country road, that night I decided to skip the medication. And while I was able to get three or four hours of sleep even without the Ambien, the next morning I woke up feeling just as frantic as ever, and more fixated than ever on Sjogren's Syndrome as the cause of this frenzy.

Journal Entry 10/4/05

"...I do have an EEG appt today at 10:00. Scared to death how bad that will be. Scared to death how bad all of this will be. I search the internet and try desperately to find some other cause for my mind's malfunction and for the damned T2 lesions on my brain—all things point to this blasted Sjogren's Syndrome however. And the prognosis for that looks so lousy. Add in menopause and the possibility of psychosis there and I'm a real mess... I'm thinking of calling the County Mental Health folks—see if they can help. It's just ridiculous for me to keep trying to go on like this. I'm lost in a fog—the boys are lost and I don't know how else to save any of us..."

It was because of how horribly lost all of us had become that, later that day, I did decide to call the local mental health department. As soon as someone picked up the phone, I started describing the details of what had been happening to me.

"…and then the doctors discovered these lesions in my brain," I said nervously. "I'm afraid I might be dying, and I have a lot of anxiety. I was wondering if there's anything you could do to help me."

After listening to my long and arduous tale of woe, the woman who answered the phone very kindly explained that while she would be happy to try and help with my anxiety, there was nothing she or anyone at the mental health department could do about my physical problems or the lesions.

"I'm sorry," she said. "For that you're going to need to seek the advice of a qualified medical doctor."

I'm not at all sure what it was I expected the people at the mental health department to say when I called that morning, or what it was I needed to hear—maybe some confirmation as to whether I had lost my mind or whether it was still intact. Certainly, there wasn't anyone there who could tell me that, not after only a five-minute phone call. Although the woman's offer to help with my anxiety did sound appealing, knowing it would probably mean more medication and more medication crises, I decided to forgo the mental health route for the time being and, instead, to take the woman's suggestion about seeking "the advice of a qualified medical doctor" by heading off to my EEG appointment.

****

As soon as my mother and I got to the hospital, one of the technicians from the radiology department led me into a small room where she began attaching all of these electrodes to my scalp, attaching them with some sort of sticky gel. Once the electrodes were in place, I sat in a chair as instructed, closed my eyes, and waited for the test to finish. I'm not sure whether it was the darkened room or if it really was because of some sort of inner darkness, but throughout the entire twenty minutes or so that the EEG was running, all I could feel inside my head was that heavy, black curtain that had descended over my mind a few days earlier.

What if there aren't any brain waves? I thought, struggling to feel something beyond the blackness. *What if the technician looks at the results and doesn't see any brain waves at all? What will happen to me then?*

To my surprise, the technician didn't seem to be at all alarmed by anything she saw on the monitor during my test; not once did I hear her gasp "Oh, my God!" or "This is awful!" while the EEG was running. Instead, once the test was over, she simply removed the electrodes and told me she'd have the neurologist take a look at the results once he got back from vacation.

"You'd probably be safe to make an appointment with him sometime early next week," she said. "Monday or Tuesday...I'm sure he'll have his report finished by then."

Even though it sounded like a horribly long time to have to wait for my results, a whole week, I couldn't help hoping that this was the doctor who would finally be able to save me. Surely, a doctor who specializes in nervous system disorders would be able to figure out what was going on inside my brain. Once he had a chance to look at the EEG together with the

MRI and the lesions, certainly this neurologist would be able to give me some kind of diagnosis. At least I prayed he would.

On the way home from the hospital, I decided to take a quick detour through a small cemetery I'd noticed just a few blocks down the road. What I was hoping to find there, I'm not really sure. Over the years, I had spent many, many hours walking and driving through cemeteries, some that were well kept and others that were withered with age. I had to wonder, was it the solitude of the cemeteries that drew me—the peace and the stillness—or was there something beyond the tranquility I was hoping to find there, something else tucked between the graves?

Neither my mother nor I said much that morning as I wound the car along the narrow road that slinked through the acre or so of gravesites. As we started toward the back, in the middle of a small hill I spotted a tombstone etched with the name of a woman I could see died while in her late-forties.

Like me, I thought. *This woman was in her late-forties like me. I wonder if she died from an illness similar to mine, some sort of midlife mayhem.*

As we got closer to the woman's grave, I noticed something that looked like a short poem engraved on the tombstone and stopped the car so I could read it.

> "The Light of God Surrounds Me.
> The Love of God Enfolds Me.
> The Power of God Protects Me.
> The Presence of God Watches Over Me.
> Wherever I am, God is."
>   *Prayer for Protection, by James Dillet Freeman, 1941*

As soon as I finished reading, I knew that these were the words I wanted to have etched into my own tombstone. Prayer had always been such an important part of my life, even during times like this when God seemed to be so very far away and unreachable. What better inscription was there to escort me into the afterlife than this simple affirmation of God's unfailing presence? Wanting to be sure that I remembered every word exactly as it was written, I scribbled the epitaph down on a scrap of paper and stuffed it into my purse.

****

Nearly every day since my episode on the hallway floor and my middle-of-the-night trip to the ER, David and Jonathan had been trying to reach my husband. He hadn't called or emailed since he left for Europe on September 21st, and at fifteen years-old my sons were able to see that I was in serious trouble, that we were all in serious trouble and needed help beyond what my mother was able to give. Since he was due to arrive back in the country on October 4th, however, that afternoon my husband did answer his cell phone. Finally, my sons and I were able to begin explaining to him everything that had been happening at home: the episode on the hallway floor, the ER, the MRI, the EEG—my terror and my sons' fear.

As soon as my husband got back to the house, my mother quickly packed her things and returned to her own home, leaving me to continue my search for sanity in the arms of my crumbling marriage. Was this even possible? Just a little over a month earlier, my husband and I were barely even speaking to each other and, for years, rarely saw each other for more than a few days out of every month—not quite the foundation on which to try to rebuild my sanity. I had been betrayed by this man in numerous ways over the years, and had listened to him lie about these betrayals numerous times, even in counseling. Although by the time of my crisis my husband and I had been married for nearly eight years, living together for ten, and had known each other for over a quarter of a century, even in good health we had failed miserably at creating a life together, miserably. How could I possibly expect to create a life with him now with my health falling apart?

****

I was so desperate to fix whatever had gone haywire inside my brain that in addition to all of my other medical appointments, I had also arranged to see a neurosurgeon later that week, on October 6th. That's right—a neuro*surgeon*. Of course, this wasn't my doctor's idea. It was my own brainchild, my hope being to get rid of the lesions and my lunacy with one swift slice of the surgeon's scalpel. Nothing else seemed to be working, and it felt as if I was losing more of my mind every day…every hour…every minute. As far as I could see, time was running out and running out fast, so I had to do something.

Since the receptionist at the neurosurgeon's office had asked me to bring the results from my MRI with me, before going to my appointment, I headed back to my local hospital to collect my films. As I was walking back out to my car, I could hardly stand the suspense of wondering what I would find when I opened the large manila envelope the hospital technician had given me.

Could there be something the doctors aren't telling me? I wondered. *Could there be something even worse than the lesions destroying my mind?*

As soon as I got in the car, I tore into the envelope and pulled out the report that described the results of the MRI:

"History: Hypertension. Shaking.

The cerebral ventricles are normal in size and position. No intra-axial or extra-axial mass is demonstrated.

A few nonspecific foci of abnormal increased T2 signal intensity in the subcortical white matter are most likely due to old microvascular ischemia. Other possibilities including demyelinating processes or gliosis cannot be excluded."

That's it? I thought. *Hypertension and shaking? Why doesn't the report say anything about my confusion or my madness, my racing pulse? Microvascular ischemia? Demyelinating processes? What about Cerebral Vasculitis and Sjogren's Syndrome?*

As far as I was concerned, this report didn't offer any more of an explanation about what was causing my "disturbances" than all the other tests I'd had. Besides the description of my lesions, it seemed to be nothing but conjecture and second-best guesses. Wanting to know more, I pulled the films out of the envelope and began searching for the lesions myself.

Where are they? Where are they?

I have to admit, to my laywoman's eye the lesions were a little difficult to find, and, once I was able to locate them, I could hardly believe how small and innocent they looked—a spot here and a spot there, all white and hazy against a grainy background of gray and black. I had to wonder how these tiny spots could be causing so much trouble in my body and in my brain, and yet, here they were—the only physical abnormality revealed by my numerous tests. I didn't care what the doctors said. Somehow, I had to get rid of them.

I wasn't at the neurosurgeon's office even ten minutes when I was told me he refused to see me. As soon as he looked at the results from my MRI, he told his receptionist to inform me there wasn't anything he could do to help me.

"I'm sorry," the receptionist said from behind her desk. "This isn't the type of condition that calls for surgery or for a neurosurgeon. It's something that's more in line with the skills of a neurologist, someone who deals with brain disorders that can be treated by non-surgical methods."

With my hopes for a quick surgical fix dashed and the neurologist from my EEG still on vacation, I didn't waste any time at all planning my next move. Before the receptionist could even hand me my bill, I was already asking (okay, begging) if it would be possible for me to make an appointment with the neurologist on staff in that office, the neurosurgeon's partner, a physician I learned was not only a neurologist but a psychiatrist as well.

This is it! I thought. *Finally, a doctor who'll be able to tell me whether there really is something physically wrong with me, or if I'm psychotic.*

After making a few phone calls to check the neurologist's schedule, the receptionist informed me that she'd be able to give me an appointment for the next day, October 7th.

****

Journal Entry 10/7/05

"Good Lord, here I am, alive still another day! Don't know whether or not I'm still sane. For some reason, I've woken up feeling a strange sort of calm—a worsening dementia? Or a step toward healing? Perhaps that's a sign that I truly am going—that my mind is so far gone that I can no longer even panic over my ailment or situation—the loss of my sanity and/or my life. Just such a calm, a silence from which I can still write, thank God. Perhaps it is the beginning of the end or perhaps it's the eye of the storm..."

As I walked into the neurologist's office, I could see the images from my MRI tacked up on a brightly lit screen, the lesions so much easier for me to see now that I had looked at them so many times. After inviting my husband and me to have a seat, the neurologist began explaining why he too believed the lesions were not in any way the cause of my "disturbances."

"Then what's wrong with me?" I pleaded. "My heart never stops pounding. My blood pressure is always high, and I keep shaking all the time. There must be something causing all of this. And there must be something causing the lesions."

The neurologist looked at the screen and began studying the images of my brain.

"The lesions could have been caused by some kind of traumatic head injury," he said. "Some blow to the head." In a tone that seemed almost half-joking, the neurologist then looked back at me and asked, "Did someone hit you in the head?"

All at once, I could feel everything inside of me beginning to speed up as I struggled to race beyond the neurologist's question. Every part of my body seemed to be pounding now—my heart, my head, even the tips of my fingers. Behind me, I could hear my husband mumble something about the childhood beating I had told him about several years earlier.

"Maybe it has something to do with your mother," he said. "That time she hit you in the head with her shoe."

My mind and body reeling, I tried not to hear what my husband was saying, and tried even harder to will the neurologist into not hearing it. Everything about that incident had come to me from such a strange place inside my mind, through dreams and brief flashes of memory. How could I possibly trust those images now with my mind falling apart, and with my mother sitting in the waiting room? Instead of answering the neurologist's question, I just stood there, trembling the way I always did. That's when the neurologist took off his glasses, looked me straight in the eye and asked me something even more startling—

"Were you ever molested?"

I could hardly believe the questions this neurologist was asking me! How could he possibly know these things about my life, and how could he have connected them to my "disturbances"? As I struggled to make my own connections— connections between the events of my past and my present chaos—it seemed everyone in the room was waiting for my answer: the neurologist, my husband, even me. It was a moment of truth, one that, given my rapidly deteriorating mental state, I couldn't afford to let slip by.

"Yes," I replied. "Yes, I was molested."

Although I can't remember exactly what the neurologist said once I gave him my answer, I do recall that it had something to do with how he'd seen this type of behavior before, this type of behavior and these types of symptoms and how they were often related to a history of childhood sexual abuse.

Oh, my God! I thought excitedly. *Does this mean I'm not going to die? Does this mean I'm going to live?*

I was so excited at the prospect of finally being able to abandon my self-imposed death sentence that I ran out into the waiting room and threw my arms around my mother.

"He thinks it's all because I was molested," I told her. "Everything that's been happening to me—the racing heart, the insomnia, feeling like I'm crazy—the doctor thinks it's all because I was molested!"

I believe it was because of how worried I'd been about the lesions and having not gotten the results from my EEG back yet that the neurologist then suggested we go ahead and run a second EEG there in his office, just to put my mind a bit more at ease.

"You'll feel a whole lot better once you're able to see that everything's normal," he assured me.

So, for the second time that week, a technician came in and began loading up my scalp with electrodes and sticky gel. Once everything was in place, rather than sitting upright in a chair like during my first EEG, I was instructed to lie down on an examining table for the test. Seeing how certain the neurologist seemed to be that the results would be normal, I thought I might try taking a nap while the EEG was running. After all, if it was just my abuse causing my "disturbances" and not some dreaded disease, what did I have to fear?

Comforted by this thought and by the neurologist's reassurance, once the technician finished setting up the test, I closed my eyes and tried to settle into sleep. Then, just as I was starting to doze, just as I was starting to drift off to a place of blessed relaxation and relief, I felt a familiar wave of panic shoot through my body.

Oh, my God, I thought. *Not this. Not now.*

I knew this feeling, knew it all too well, but never experienced it anywhere other than lying on my yoga mat at home. Why was it showing up here? Why now? No matter how hard I tried to make this feeling go away and no matter how hard I tried to pretend it wasn't there, for the rest of the time the EEG was running, every time I felt myself starting to relax the "twitch thing" would come and startle me back into that all-too-familiar feeling of terror.

How can this be happening? I wondered. *I thought I was fine. Everyone keeps telling me I'm fine, so why does this keep happening?*

After about thirty minutes or so of the EEG running and me trying to outrun the "twitch thing," the test was finally finished. Once the technician removed the electrodes, the neurologist asked my husband and me if we wouldn't mind stepping out of the room for a few minutes so that he and the technician could review my results. I wasn't even halfway to the door when I stopped and turned around.

"Can I watch, too?" I asked. The neurologist looked up and began studying me as intently as he had the images of my brain. "The EEG results," I said. "Can I watch them, too?"

"Um, we don't normally do that," the neurologist replied, glancing at the technician. "But…I suppose if you want to. Sure. Okay. Why not?"

In order to give themselves the best view possible of my brain waves, the neurologist and the technician each set up a chair directly in front of the computer while I sat in a chair behind them, my husband next to me. As the results from my EEG began to dance across the screen, I was amazed to see all the zig-zaggy lines indicating what was going on inside my brain, all of the lines, according to the neurologist, looking perfectly normal. Every now and then, there'd be a peak or two in the activity where the neurologist said I must have been reacting to a noise in the room or to some other distraction.

"All perfectly normal," the neurologist said again. "Perfectly normal."

I guess it must be because of my abuse then, I thought. *All of my "disturbances," they must be because of my abuse since the...*

"Whoa, look at that!" I heard the neurologist exclaim.

I must have looked away from the screen for just a second but looked back just in time to see a large dip in my brain wave activity, some sort of deep valley or gorge in the graph that fell way below the other lines, *way* below.

"Whoa, look at that one!" the neurologist said again, this time rocking back in his chair and slamming his foot down on the floor for emphasis. "I've never seen anything like it. And that one!"

It was as if they had forgotten I was even in the room, the neurologist and the technician, both of them so taken aback by the abnormalities in my EEG that they could hardly contain their excitement. The whole time my brain waves continued to dance across the screen, dip after monstrous dip and valley after monstrous valley, the two men continued their ooh's and aah's, with me sitting behind them, trembling in fear.

Is there even any hope for me? I wondered. *Anything that can save me...anything that can save my sons?*

As soon as the EEG finished running, the first thing the neurologist did was prescribe an anti-seizure medication to control my abnormal brain activity—Lamictal.

"But shouldn't we find out what's causing the seizures first?"
I begged as I watched him scribble something across a little
white pad. "Shouldn't I wait and take something that will
fix whatever's causing the seizures? What about Sjorgren's
Syndrome? What about Cerebral Vasculitis? Shouldn't we do
a brain biopsy?" (You'd think that, by now, I would have given
up on the researching.)

To be thorough, or perhaps only to pacify me, the
neurologist agreed to run a few blood tests, insisting, once
again, that the results would be normal. After the blood had
been drawn, not knowing what else to do or what other options
I had, I reached out and picked up the prescription.

Considering all of my recent medication crises, I wasn't all
that enthusiastic about taking another drug that, in my mind,
would do nothing more than cover up my "disturbances." I
wanted to know what was causing them, damn it! I wanted
to know what was causing the brain wave abnormalities, the
lesions, the "twitch thing," the God-awful smell, the insomnia,
the racing heart, the skyrocketing blood pressure, the shaking,
the trembling, and, most of all, I wanted to know what was
making me feel like I was losing my mind! I was more than
willing to take a medication that would fix whatever was
causing all of this, but no one seemed to be able to tell me what
that was.

"We'll start you on this medication over the weekend," the
neurologist said as I was leaving. "Then come back on Monday
and we'll run a twenty-four hour EEG. We'll be able to know
more after that."

I don't remember what my husband and I talked about on
the way home. I do know that he was supposed to leave for

another trip the next day, on the 8th, but now with the results of my EEG being so bizarre, that was out of the question. Before going back to the house, we stopped at a local pharmacy to pick up the medication the neurologist seemed to believe would have me seizure-free in no time. As usual, I wasn't nearly as convinced. As soon as my husband and I got home, I rushed into the house, turned on the computer, and began looking up the side effects for Lamictal before I would even open the bottle. Although there were many side effects listed on the website, side effects that included anxiety, insomnia, and confusion (really?), it was the rare but sometimes fatal side effect, a rash known as Stevens-Johnson Syndrome, that did it for me.

Is this doctor serious? I thought as I read and then reread the details about the sometimes-fatal side effect. *There's no way I'm taking something that could kill me. No way!*

And so, as with the Xanax, the Inderal, the Ambien, and the Buspar, I refused to take the Lamictal, and demanded that my husband return it to the pharmacy for disposal.

Alone in the house after my husband left, I felt trapped, trapped inside a mind and body I could no longer recognize, that were both falling apart, and, no matter how hard I tried and no matter which doctor I went to see, there was nothing I could do to rescue either one. Bit by bit, I could feel myself shutting out the outside world and spiraling deeper and deeper into my inner world, deeper into my chaos. It just didn't make sense to continue looking outside for help when there was obviously nothing there that could save me. But then, why look inside? What could I possibly have had inside of me that could?

Journal Entry 10/8/05

"...Not so good at the Neuro—some weird stuff on the EEG...How to sleep now? How to heal? How to die? This is truly like torture—God won't help me and won't kill me. Half of my mind is gone and I have to sit by and watch it go. Why God? Why did you choose to destroy my mind and not give me something simpler to die from—a sane death at least..."

****

While my husband and I were at the neurologist's office that day watching my bizarre brain waves dance across the computer screen, my sons were at school, both of them participating in Ag Day—a town-wide event celebrating the pride of our small farming community. Each year during the two-day celebration, our town is overflowing with events like barbeques and tractor pulls, Crazy Creature contests, and displays of local produce. Also as part of the celebration, the students and staff at the local middle/high school get to take time off from their studies and spend their Friday afternoon immersed in a bustle of school-oriented Ag Day activities, activities such as the Parade of Colors, relay races, and Frisbee Football. It was during an especially competitive game of Frisbee Football that while diving for the Frisbee, Jonathan crashed into another student, fell to the ground, and injured his wrist. It didn't seem to be broken at the time and the school nurse assured him she didn't think it was, but, by the next morning, it still wasn't getting any better so I knew I had to do something.

For the life of me, I couldn't figure out how I was going to get Jonathan to a doctor. My mind was so jumbled—I had no idea what had to be done first, or last, or even how I was supposed to figure any of that out. By this time, I was having a hard enough time trying to manage everyday tasks, tasks like taking a shower, shopping for food, and even remembering to turn off the oven. Any new task added to this mix seemed impossible. I was beginning to feel like I was in one of those cartoons where the sidewalk keeps disappearing from under the character's feet. For months, I had been running and running to try to save myself and not getting anywhere, and now I had to do something to help my son.

How am I going to do this? I wondered, my mind a cluttered mess. *How?*

It was raining outside that afternoon, pouring, and, at some point, I can remember becoming so frustrated by my inability to think straight that I ran outside and started stomping around in the puddles in my backyard. I don't believe there were any words with this stomping, only the frantic pounding of my bare feet against the wet earth and my fingers tearing at my matted hair. Through the window, I could see my sons watching and worrying, the expression on their faces seeming to beg the question, "What are we going to do with Mom?" When I finally realized how useless all of my stomping was, I came back into the house, threw myself down onto the living room floor and did something I hadn't done in years—I lifted an angry fist to my head.

"Mom stop," David pleaded. "Stop…you'll become delusional."

"I already am," I replied, my voice a mixture of panic and surrender. "I already am," I said again before lowering my hand to my lap.

Later that afternoon and with my husband's help, I was able to get Jonathan to the ER where, after a few x-rays, the doctors discovered that he did have a broken wrist.

What kind of mother overlooks this kind of injury? I asked myself...berated myself. *What kind of mother have I become? What kind of person?*

With no orthopedist available at the hospital, the doctors informed me that I'd need to make an appointment with the orthopedist's office the following Monday to have the fracture set.

"It's not a serious break," the ER doctor assured me. "I'm sure he'll be fine until then."

Remembering that Monday was the same day I was scheduled to have my twenty-four hour EEG, I flew into a whole new panic. Since the two offices were located just a few blocks away from each other and at least thirty miles from my home, I knew the whole family would probably have to be there when I saw the neurologist—me, my husband, and my sons. I couldn't help wondering what would happen if the neurologist discovered something even more bizarre going on inside my brain. What would that do to my already frantic mind? What would that do to my sons?

****

Over the three or four days before Jonathan broke his wrist, I had been growing more and more obsessed about a whole new "disturbance" I seemed to be having, a "disturbance" that involved my eyes—my pupils. For some reason, they had begun to look a whole lot smaller than they normally looked, smaller and eerily lifeless.

I even look like I'm psychotic now, I can remember thinking. *My eyes, they look so flat…so emotionless…so dead.*

From what I could tell, it seemed that my pupils had completely stopped responding to the dark. They didn't seem to be dilating at all anymore, and, as with all of my other "disturbances," I was desperate to find out why. Since I'd already spent more than enough time sitting in the emergency room, I decided to devise my own test to try to figure out whether this new "disturbance" was all in my mind, or if there really was something wrong with my eyes. All I would need for this test was a flashlight, a small hand mirror, and a dark room. The flashlight and mirror I was able to locate easily enough— one in the kitchen drawer and the other in the bathroom closet. It was the dark room that had me stumped. After much confused and frantic deliberation, I finally figured it out.

I know! I thought triumphantly. *I'll go into the hallway closet! That'll work! I'll just have to wait until the sun goes down so it'll be dark in there.*

Later that night, armed with my flashlight and mirror, I stepped into the closet and slowly pulled the door shut behind me.

Well, look-y there, I can remember thinking as I peered into the darkness. *I didn't have to wait until nighttime after all. It's always dark in here when you close the door. Huh. Imagine that.*

Once I had shut myself in the closet, I held the mirror in front of my face and began switching the flashlight on and off while aiming the beam directly into my eyes. I'd do this suddenly and quickly in the hope of being able to catch my pupils off-guard, to be able to see whether or not they had been dilated the moment before the light hit them. Much like when I was checking my blood sugar and blood pressure back in

September, I would perform this flashlight maneuver over, and over, and over.

Were my pupils dilated just now? I couldn't really tell. Or was it just my imagination, my wishful thinking? Let me try again…

…and again, and again, and again.

Unsure of what I was seeing there in the dark, I'd keep flashing the light into my eyes until, finally, there'd be nothing left for me to do but give up. A few hours later, sometimes only a few minutes later, I'd be right back in the closet, holding the mirror in front of me and starting the whole process over again.

On. Off. On. Off.

Were my pupils dilated just now or weren't they? Were they or weren't they? Were they or weren't they? Were they or…

Maddening…all of it, simply maddening.

Journal Entry 10/10/05

"Terrified for my life—for my sanity and now my eyesight as well. So much loss so quickly. Only hope my sons remember me the way I was. For that reason alone I'd rather go quickly—just move on and let the boys get on with their lives…so awful to have to live out my Dad's legacy. So sad…"

****

Sometime early Monday afternoon, my husband, my sons, and I all got into the car and headed off to the appointments we had scheduled for the day, the appointment for my EEG the first on our list. Since this was to be the third EEG I'd had in less than a week, I knew the installation procedure well—more electrodes and more sticky gel. This time, however, since the EEG wasn't going to be running for a mere twenty to thirty minutes but a full twenty-four hours, the technician also gave me a little blue beanie to wear over the electrodes along with some sort of recording device I was instructed to wear strapped across my back. It was cumbersome, yes, but even more distressing was how all of this equipment seemed to make me feel as if I was wearing some kind of outer declaration of everything that had gone wrong inside my head, a banner that screamed, "Hey, look everyone! I've lost my marbles!" There was no use trying to escape it now, no use trying to hide what was now so obvious. For the next twenty-four hours, instead of carrying my chaos around inside of me, in my heart and in my head where no one else could see it, I would be dragging it around outside of me as well, outside for the whole world to see.

Once the technician finished setting up the EEG, he led me into the neurologist's office where there was still the medication issue to be dealt with, the medication I still refused to take.

"It's such a rare occurrence," the neurologist argued as we discussed the sometimes-fatal side effect of Lamictal, the Stevens-Johnson Syndrome. "It really isn't something you should worry about."

"I don't care. I'm not taking it," I said, holding my ground. "I have enough wrong with me already, and besides, we don't even know if it'll help."

Looking somewhat perplexed, the neurologist got out of his chair and came around his desk to stand next to me by the door.

"I prescribe more of this type of medication than any other doctor in the area," he said, "and I've had a lot of good results with my patients."

"I'm sure you have," I replied. "But I…"

The neurologist then went on to tell me about a certain patient he remembered having, a young man who had to drop out of college because his seizures were so bad. According to the neurologist, once he started taking Lamictal this young man was able to go back to school, finish his bachelor's degree, and was currently thinking about applying to medical school.

"Like you, he complained of smelling something odd," the neurologist recounted. "He said he would often smell something just before having a seizure."

Although everything the neurologist was saying did sound intriguing, especially the part about the young man smelling something the way I so often did, I still wasn't convinced about taking the medication.

"Okay, then why don't we try Keppra," the neurologist suggested. "With your symptoms, I think that would be the next best medication for you."

Unbeknownst to the neurologist, I had just spent a good part of the weekend sitting behind my computer researching various anti-seizure medications and their side effects, and had already made up my mind about which one I would be willing to consider taking.

"What about Neurontin?" I asked, countering the neurologist's Keppra. "From what I read it seems to have fewer side effects than the other medications."

The neurologist stared at me as if I were some perplexing puzzle he'd been working on.

"No," he replied sternly. "No. Neurontin wouldn't be right for you at all. We'll stick with the Keppra for now and see what the twenty-four hour results tell us."

With my twenty-four hour EEG up and running and a prescription for the new anti-seizure medication in my hand, my husband, my sons, and I all hurried off to our next appointment—the orthopedist's office where we were scheduled to have Jonathan's fracture set.

As soon as we walked into the waiting room, it seemed as if every head in the place turned to look at me. Had I become paranoid or were these people really staring at me? And, if they were staring, was it because of the EEG equipment, or was it because, like everyone else, they too had all come to the conclusion that I was some kind of "case"? Before I could decide which one it was, another all too familiar "disturbance" began demanding my attention.

Zsst.

What was that?

Zsst...zap, zap.

Was that one of those electric jolts?

Zap. Zap. Zap.

Oh, my God, it was. Why is this happening to me now? I asked myself. *Why? Is it something in the EEG equipment? Something in my brain?*

Shaky and embarrassed, I walked up to the reception area. "My son Jonathan has an appointment at 3:00," I said, trying to control my fear.

"Oh, yes. I see," the receptionist replied as she shuffled through some paperwork on her desk. "Do you have a referral from Jonathan's primary care physician?"

"A referral?" I repeated, my thoughts even more wild and disjointed than usual. "Um, no. I don't. Do I need one?"

Zap. Zap.

"Yes. I'm afraid we're going to need to see a referral before Jonathan can see the doctor," the receptionist said matter-of-factly, and then turned her attention to the next patient on line.

What am I going to do now? I thought. *How am I supposed to get a referral? What's wrong with this woman? Can't she see that I've lost my mind?*

Since I knew there wasn't any way I was going to be able to remember the doctor's telephone number, I asked the receptionist if I could borrow a phone book. As soon as she handed one to me, I took it to a far corner of the waiting room, squatted down on the floor—knees to my chest like a chimpanzee—and began frantically flipping through the pages. And I thought the people in the waiting room were staring at me before!

What on earth was that doctor's name? I wondered as I tore through the large yellow book. *Is he in a group of doctors, or is it a solo practice? And how do you spell "physician" anyway?*

The whole time I was flipping through the pages, I could feel those electric jolts still tearing through my body.

Zap! Zap! ZAP!

At the same time, it seemed as if all the lights in the waiting room were suddenly switching in and out of varying degrees of brightness.

Light. Dark. Light. Dark.

Zap! Zap! ZAP!

Oh, my God, what's happening to me? I thought, still trying to search through the phone book. *Am I dying? Am I dying right now? But I can't. I have to do this. I have to take care of Jonathan. I can't die now. Please, God. Please.*

Whether through the hard-headedness of my madness or the staunch determination of motherhood, even with the zapping and flashing, somehow, I was able to find the telephone number and get the referral. I can remember holding onto the telephone as if for dear life while I spoke to the nurse, doing everything in my power to sound as clear and coherent as possible.

"Yes. That's right. I need a referral for Jonathan, for his broken wrist."

Zap. Zap, zap, ZAP!

Once I had the referral, with everyone in the waiting room still staring at me (okay, maybe I was a bit paranoid), I followed my son into the examining room. As soon as I sat down, I could almost hear what the doctor was thinking—

"Poor kid. I can tell just by looking at her that his mother is definitely some kind of case."

Since I had been to see this particular orthopedist several times over the years for my sons' boyhood injuries and had often enjoyed our friendly chats, I couldn't help noticing how much things had changed since the last time I saw him, how much *I* had changed. Was it because of how embarrassed I felt or because of the zapping that, instead of chatting, I spent most of the appointment staring at the floor in silence?

Zap. Zap, zap, zap.

By the time the orthopedist finished setting Jonathan's wrist, the zapping and flashing had me so out of my mind with fear that as soon as my husband, my sons, and I stepped out into the lobby, I lost it.

"Oh, my God, I'm dying," I said. "I'm dying right now... RIGHT NOW! Oh, my God. Someone help me. Please, help me! What am I going to do? I'm dying! I'm dying!"

Having become somewhat used to my "dying right now" tirades, my sons and my husband did their best to console me and then hurried me back out to the car. Even the ground beneath my feet seemed to be shifting as I struggled to make my way across the parking lot, my thoughts wildly panicked and yet strangely calm all at the same time. I could almost hear all of my inner "others" arguing among themselves over what my state of mind should be.

I'm so scared, I could sense one part of me screaming.

Not me, another part seemed to chide. *I feel as calm as can be. Look at all the rest of you, panicking like a bunch of chickens.*

Why don't you stop arguing and do something? yet another part of me begged. *What if I really am dying?*

With the electrodes still stuck to my scalp and the recording equipment still strapped across my back, I shuddered to think how all of this chaos was affecting my brain waves, what havoc it must have been causing on my EEG.

This is going to be bad, I thought. *Really bad, but at least everyone will finally be able to see how far gone I am.*

On the way home from the orthopedist's, my husband decided to stop at a mini-mart for gas, and, while we were there, I decided it was high time I threw my years-long severely restrictive diet overboard. Picking up my purse, I marched into the mini-mart and bought myself a bag of potato chips—chips of the best-known baked variety.

"What are you doing?" wailed my sons the instant I came out of the store.

Over the years, my sons had watched me slowly and carefully whittle my diet down to the mere four or five foods my body seemed willing to tolerate, and now, here I was eating potato chips!

"What are you doing?" they demanded again.

"It doesn't matter," I said as I slipped another chip into my mouth. "What I eat and what I don't eat... none of it makes any difference. Look at me for God's sake! Look at me with this thing on my head! Nothing I do is helping—nothing. I just keep getting worse and worse. What does it matter what I eat?"

While I was talking, everything around me began to feel strangely crystal-like, translucent and sharp, and seemed to be breaking apart into tiny fragments. I could almost hear it. Was that me breaking apart or was it still just my mind? Whatever it was, I could hardly stand another minute of it. If I was going to die, then I wished I would just hurry up and get it over with already. God! This hovering between life and death was getting worse than maddening. It was getting to where some part of me wanted to do something to help tip the scales toward the latter.

By the time we got home, I had managed to pull myself together enough to run inside and start looking up the side effects for the neurologist's new medication. In addition to the severe allergic reactions and behavioral changes listed on the website (didn't I already have enough of those?), there was another far more concerning side effect that could occur while taking Keppra. It was a side effect that, given my current state of mind, could prove to be far more threatening than even the Stevens-Johnson Syndrome of Lamictal—thoughts of suicide.

But I'm already having thoughts of suicide, I thought. *What am I going to do now?*

The thoughts I had begun to have about killing myself were becoming too real and too frequent to ignore, and yet, for some reason, I still wasn't able to acknowledge them to anyone or

even access them fully. A thought here and a thought there—
every once in a while some image of a woman jumping off of
a bridge or walking into a nearby lake would just suddenly fly
into my mind and then disappear as quickly as it came…like
fireflies…like wind. Like that day back in September, I knew
it wasn't me who wanted to commit suicide, not the present-
day me. The present-day me so wanted to stay alive, to stay
alive so I could be here with my sons. All of these thoughts
about death and dying, these thoughts about suicide, had to be
coming from some other part of me, some inaccessible "other"
who was apparently growing more and more powerful by the
day. I didn't dare take a chance on giving this "other" any more
power by taking a medication that could cause me to have even
more thoughts about suicide. Although I had no idea which
way to turn or what I was going to do next, as with all of the
other medications I'd been prescribed, I refused to take the
Keppra and decided to take my chances on what the twenty-
four hour EEG might reveal.

Journal Entry 10/11/05
    "…How much do I have to lose before someone tries to
help, before my life is completely over? Wouldn't be so bad if
I were old and gray, if the boys were grown and out on their
own. Wouldn't be so bad. But this—oh this just hurts so
terribly much. So much I still wanted to do—so much that's
just so hard to do. Although it won't help, I'll still turn my
face to the heavens and beg, "Why?" And not just, "Why
me?" but "Why anyone?" Why should anyone have to lose
their minds before they die? So painful. So terribly, terribly
painful. Please dear God, still praying for a miracle…or at

the very least, peace for all of us. Peace in my dementia or in
my death—peace…"

****

A few days later, while waiting to pick my sons up at school, my husband saw that there was a message on his voicemail from the neurologist. Figuring it must have something to do with the results from my EEG, he decided to listen to it right away. What the neurologist said in his message came as such a shock to my husband that instead of just telling me what was in it, he had me listen to every word as soon as he got home.

"The EEG is all clear," I heard the neurologist's voice announce on my husband's cell phone. "Completely normal. Keep taking the medication and we'll check back in a month or so."

I was so confused by what the neurologist said in his message that I played it over a second time and then a third.

"…Completely normal…Keep taking the medication."

"…Completely normal… Keep taking the medication."

"But I never took the medication," I said, directing my bewilderment more to myself than to my husband. "I never took it."

I never took the medication the neurologist prescribed and yet, for the full twenty-four hours that the EEG was running, my brain waves didn't show so much as a single nose dive or curve, not even a blip. Everything was normal. As I stood in my kitchen, still holding my husband's cellphone to my ear, in my mind I quickly replayed some of the zapping scenes I could remember from the orthopedist's office as well as the frenzied battle I could sense between my "others" in the lobby after we left.

And nothing showed up on the EEG? I wondered. *With all of that chaos, nothing showed up?*

None of what was happening was making any sense to me. I couldn't understand how my EEG could suddenly be normal when, just a few days earlier, it was showing these horrendous dips in my brain waves; dips that were occurring every few minutes, every few seconds; dips that had even the neurologist/ psychiatrist perplexed; dips that, to me, had looked much like the languid undulations of a snake. The dips had been there. That much was certain. The question was—where had they disappeared to, and what was I going to do now?

****

After over three months of searching for some sort of diagnosis for my "disturbances," it seemed that I had reached the end of my help line. With no other medical tests I could pull out of my sleeve and no other doctors on my list, there was nothing I could do to try to save myself. Like it or not, it was time for me to come to terms with the fact that if I wasn't going to die, then this was how I was going to have to live—in this state of confused frenzy. There would be no more helping my sons with their homework, no more serving on the library board, or even balancing my checkbook. All of it, everything, had become far too overwhelming for me. If I was lucky, I might be able to throw a dinner together at the end of the day, but even that would mean we'd be eating "Jet Age Pizza" for the second, and the third, and the fourth night in a row.

It was while I was struggling to come to terms with this strange, new person I'd become that I began to notice a whole new "disturbance" beginning to emerge, a "disturbance" quite different from all the ones I had become so used to, a "disturbance" that I found to be especially disturbing—waves of intense sexual energy. Yeah, yeah, I know, many of you reading this are probably thinking, "Wow! Lucky you! Lots of sex!" But it wasn't like that at all. These were no ordinary waves of desire. They were *insanely* sexual. Or, no, what I meant to write was insane *and* sexual, a combination of energies that, for me, simply didn't mix. Because of the difficulties in my marriage, by the time of my crisis I was no longer sleeping with my husband, and didn't feel any more interested in sleeping with him or with anyone else during these waves than I had been before. For reasons that seemed to have little to do with lovemaking or lust, my body was just suddenly filled with all of this whirling, swirling sexual energy.

It was during this time of sexual overload that, one night, while out for my usual walk, I ran into a neighbor of mine. I think it was because of what I knew about this neighbor's brother having been diagnosed with schizophrenia some thirty years earlier that I thought she might be able to empathize with my concerns about my own mental state.

"I've lost my mind," I said to this neighbor while we stood chatting beneath the moon and stars. "Something's wrong with my brain. I have these lesions and I think they're making me psychotic."

"Really," my neighbor replied, eyeing me suspiciously in the glow of the streetlight.

"Yes. It's important that you tell everyone you know," I continued, "just in case I start running around without my clothes on or something, in case I start running around naked. I wouldn't want people thinking I'd do something like that while in my right mind, so make sure you tell everyone you know that I've gone crazy…just so they'll know what to expect."

We talked for a few minutes more—my neighbor and I—
about the weather and about our cats, and then I said good-
night and scurried away into the darkness toward home, sort
of like a bat scampering back to its belfry. A few days later,
through the community grapevine, I learned that a few of the
local church congregations had decided to add me to their
weekly prayer list. I could almost hear them in their well-
intentioned invocations—

"…and we pray that Lynda will be able to relocate her
sanity."

"Lord, hear our prayer."

Although my neighbor had obviously gone ahead and
announced to at least some of the folks in town that I wasn't
playing with a full deck, as time would prove, this really hadn't
been necessary. Fortunately, throughout the remaining months
that wave after wave of sexual energy continued to pulse
through my body, and wave after wave of lunacy through my
mind, somehow I was able to keep enough of my wits about me
to remember to keep my clothes on. Well, at least as far as I
know.

Journal Entry 10/13/05

*"Well here I am, still waking up every day, much to
my surprise…Still don't know what's happening in my
brain…am I dying? Am I going crazy? Do I have CNS
Vasculitis? A reaction to that doxycycline? Or do I have a
menopause psychosis? Or perhaps a psychosis related to all of
my childhood trauma? The biggest question is—will I even
know? Have been seriously considering some sort of mental
hospital, like [M's] mom when she was going through*

menopause. Just don't know what else to do or where to turn. Who would have thought I'd lose so much..."

****

With one postponed business trip after another beginning to pile up and me still not making any improvement at all with my "disturbances"—physical, emotional, or sexual—by the middle of October my husband decided it was time to take matters into his own hands. The days were fast turning into weeks, after all, and, even if only for financial reasons, he would soon need to get back on the road. It was from this urgency to get our lives back to normal as quickly as possible that on the morning of October 14th, my husband announced that he was taking me to see Dr. S., a former therapist of his. In many ways, Dr. S. also felt like a former therapist of mine, as I too had been to see him several times as part of my husband's and my attempt at "couple's therapy," a therapy that, despite Dr. S.'s diligent efforts, unfortunately didn't take. The reason for this particular visit, however, wasn't for any type of marriage or relationship counseling. It was to try to figure out whether I should continue my search for some sort of physical illness as the reason for my "disturbances," or if I should start approaching them more from a mental illness perspective—in other words, to find out once and for all whether I had lost my mind.

As I stepped inside Dr. S.' office, I could see that everything was still pretty much the same as the last time I'd been there—subdued walls and carpet with just a few pictures hanging to offset the simplicity of the decor, pictures of some sort of other-consciousness realms. (Or were they images of outer space?) In one corner, I could see the infamous sand-table still standing in its usual spot, a sand-filled tray where clients could come in and construct scenes from the innermost realms of their psyches—scenes from battlefields, scenes from family gatherings—all of the "toys" used to create these scenes lined up on a set of shelves along the opposite wall.

Once my husband and I were settled in our usual spots, Dr. S. came in and took his seat across from us. Like the room, Dr. S. looked pretty much the same as I remembered—a closely cropped beard, whiter now that several years had passed, and a demeanor so open and welcoming it made any therapy session with him feel like chatting with an old friend.

"So, what's been going on?" Dr. S. asked, studying me from behind a pair of wire-framed glasses. "Why are you here today, Lynda?"

Knowing my husband had already told Dr. S. quite a bit about my condition, I wasn't sure where to start.

"Something's happened," I began. "Something's happened to my brain. I have these lesions, and there's some kind of slowing on my EEG. My heart keeps pounding and sometimes my blood pressure goes all the way up to 178/100. I have terrible insomnia. Some nights I don't sleep at all...and I keep shaking all the time. Look!"

I stopped talking just long enough to hold my hand out in front of me so Dr. S. could see it tremble.

"And my eyes," I continued. "I don't think my pupils are dilating anymore. They're always so small now, small and constricted. Maybe that's why I'm having such a hard time seeing. Whenever I try to look at something, like now when I try to look at your face, something happens on the right side

of my head. It feels like it's in a vice and you look all strange…
fuzzy…far away."

I could see that Dr. S. was doing his darnedest to try to
figure out what was going on with me and wondered if there
was anything I could do to help. Was I telling him everything
I could about my "disturbances," everything that was important
about them? Or was there something I was missing, something
I was still missing even after all these years? Looking back,
I could remember the many times my husband and I had sat
in Dr. S.' office before, times when I would start shaking so
violently I could hardly stay in my chair. And now, here it
was so many years later, and I was still shaking. Was there
something I was missing…something about my life I still
needed to remember?

Once I finished telling Dr. S. everything I could think of
about my "disturbances" as well as everything the doctors
seemed to think about them, he was ready to give us his
assessment. Since the tests I'd been having did indicate some
very real physical abnormalities (the lesions in my brain and my
slowing brain waves), and since my "disturbances" did seem to
be mostly physical (my racing heart, soaring blood pressure, and
shrunken pupils), Dr. S. felt that I should continue my efforts to
try to find a physical cause for my maladies, at least for the time
being.

"And since you haven't been having the best of luck getting
a diagnosis locally," he added, "why not try a hospital in one of
the nearby cities? Maybe someone there will be able to zero in
on something the doctors here have been missing."

See, I thought triumphantly. *See, Dr. S. thinks there's
something physically wrong with me too, so that must be it! It must
be!*

As soon as my husband and I got back into the car, he looked over at me and, with a heavy sigh, dropped his hands into his lap and shook his head. Was it because of how difficult I was making all of our lives, how difficult I was making *his* life that he seemed so exasperated with me? Or was it because of how certain he'd been that Dr. S. would draw a much different conclusion about my "disturbances"? I had to wonder, what conclusion had my husband drawn? What did he think was the cause of my confusion and fear, of my many years of trembling?

****

It was raining outside the next morning as my husband and I started getting ready to leave for the hospital. Certain the doctors there would find something wrong with me, something serious enough to admit me, I packed a small overnight bag.

"I don't know if I'll be able to come home today," I said to my sons while I was packing. "I might have to stay at the hospital, but I'll call you later. I will. I'll call."

As I wandered around my room trying to figure out what bits and pieces of my life I should bring with me, what bits and pieces of my life that might have survived the madness, I noticed my guitar standing over in one corner. Although I'd been playing the guitar and singing for over thirty-five years, somehow, with all the chaos of my "disturbances," I'd lost track of the music…pushed it away. I could remember trying to play one day during the summer, late August I think it was when, all of a sudden, from somewhere deep inside of me I felt this enormous surge of anger rising to the surface. Right in the middle of playing, I began to feel like I wanted to hurt someone—to punch and kick and scream. The anger had risen up so suddenly, I had no idea where it was coming from or what to do with it. The longer I continued to play, the stronger the anger seemed to become. Finally, terrified by what was happening and by what I might do, I stopped playing and rushed out of my room. The instant I did, the anger disappeared—poof, just like that, as if someone had flipped a switch. I hadn't touched my guitar since that day, and now, not knowing how long I'd have to stay in the hospital or if I would ever come home, I thought it was high time I did.

As I picked up the guitar and slung the strap over my shoulder, I began searching my mind for a song I might want to play—some lyric or tune from my saner days I might want to sing but found nothing there, nothing but that cursed blackness. I tried again. Still nothing.

I've been singing these songs for years, I thought anxiously, *for decades, and now I can't remember any of them? No doctor is going to tell me there isn't anything wrong with me. I've lost my mind, damn it! I've lost my music and my mind!*

After standing in the middle my room with the guitar for what seemed like hours, I finally found a piece of a song I could remember, just a few measures hanging from the wreckage of my chaos and began to play. Although I don't recall which song it was that I played that morning (Was it James Taylor's *Fire and Rain* or something by Judy Collins?), I do know that it was the only song I could remember, so, once I finished, I put the guitar away and continued packing. But even in those few words I was able to sing, I could hear that there was something strangely different about my voice—some exacting vibrato, a vibrato so strong it sounded almost like an echo, or maybe another voice. Could that echo have been the voices of my "others," my "others" struggling to be heard?

As soon as my husband and I got to the hospital, we went directly to the ER where one of the nurses asked us to sign in and explain a little bit about why we were there.

"There's something wrong with my autonomic nervous system," I said to the nurse. "All of my bodily functions seem to have gone haywire—my heart rate, my blood pressure, my nerve synapses. Everything seems to be misfiring. I think there's something wrong with my autonomic nervous system."

The nurse stood up and glanced at the sign-in sheet. "Are you a doctor?" she asked.

Embarrassed by the nurse's question, I stopped talking and looked down at the floor. Was I being too technical again, too sterile and removed? I tried shifting gears so I would sound less formal, less delusional.

"No," I replied, looking back at the nurse. "No, I'm not. I've just been doing a lot of reading…researching to try to find out what's wrong with me." I held out the large manila envelope with the results from my MRI. "I've also got these lesions in my brain," I continued. "I was hoping someone here might be able to tell me what's causing them."

The nurse took the envelope and scribbled something down on one of the folders she had tucked under her arm. Was I imagining things or had this woman too already come to the conclusion that I was some kind of "case"?

"Have a seat in the waiting room and someone will be with you shortly," the nurse said, and then disappeared down the hall.

As I sat down in the waiting room, I could see that there was a large T.V. playing over in one corner. Desperate to have something to distract me from all of my inner chaos, I tried watching whatever was on, some sort of news program I think it was, but, just like at home, nothing on the screen seemed to be making any sense. To me, it was nothing but a jumble of images and words that I could no longer connect to. It wasn't that I couldn't understand the words. It was as if they weren't even there, like they were playing on some radio frequency that was too far out of my range and coming in as nothing but static. Wanting to find something to help take my mind off whatever medical mayhem lay ahead, I picked up a magazine and began thumbing through the pages. Just then, a nurse appeared in the doorway.

"Lynda. Lynda…if you'll follow me, please."

My husband and I followed the nurse down a long hallway and into one of the examining rooms. After checking my vital signs—blood pressure, pulse, and temperature, all of which were elevated—the nurse handed me a hospital gown.

"Go ahead and put this on," she said. "And then have a seat on the bed. I'm sure the doctor will be right with you."

Once I had managed to get myself out of my clothes and into the gown, instead of sitting on the bed as instructed, I crawled all the way into it and pulled the sheets around me. They felt so warm and crisp and clean. I didn't want to ever have to come out from under them. I didn't want to ever have to come out and face whatever horrid thing was happening to my mind, whatever horrid thing I still believed was killing me.

"I just finished looking at your MRI," a doctor said as he dashed into the room. He was a young doctor, young with short dark hair and brown eyes that seemed never to settle on anyone as he spoke. "I really don't think the lesions have anything to do with the symptoms you're describing," he continued. "And I don't think they're anything for you to worry about."

I watched the doctor then lift his hand and start pointing to various parts of his own head as he began describing the locations of my lesions.

"There aren't too many of them," he noted, "just a few here, here, here, and here."

Although I'm sure this gesture was meant to comfort me in some way, all the doctor managed to do was send me into a whole new panic thinking there were even more lesions in my brain than I thought there were.

Oh, my God, I thought nervously. *They're all over my head! That must mean I really am dying!*

Wanting the doctor to have as much information as possible about what was going on inside my brain so that he could make as accurate a diagnosis as possible, I started telling him about the EEG and the slowing brain waves, about the seizures and the medications the neurologist wanted me to take for them, the Lamictal and the Keppra. The doctor stopped me before I could finish.

"Seizures are when brain activity speeds up," he said matter-of-factly. "Not when it slows down. Those aren't seizures you're having."

Although I was doing my best to try to keep up with everything the doctor was saying, it seemed that only part of me was there in the room listening and that all these other parts of me were off doing something else, something to avoid the harsh hospital lights and the harsh hospital conversations. Before I could gather enough of these parts together to ask what my slowing brain waves were if not your typical seizure, the doctor was gone. Although a nurse did come in a few times to assure me that the doctor was off consulting with some specialist about my MRI and EEG and that he'd soon be back, he never returned. For hours, my husband and I waited, and for hours, I held onto the fragile hope that, at some point, either the doctor or the specialist would burst into the room and shout, "Eureka! We know what's wrong with you!" But that never happened. Every now and then, in an effort to convince myself that, like so many doctors had already told me, there really wasn't anything wrong with me, I'd rush into the bathroom to check my eyes.

Damn it, I'd think each time I looked in the mirror. *There is something wrong with me. Look at my pupils. They look so dead! Why isn't anyone else able to see it? I'm not in there anymore, I tell you! I'm not in there!*

After spending most of the afternoon lying on the bed, teetering between feelings of hope and hopelessness, I asked my husband if he could go to the nurse's station to see if he could find out what had happened to the doctor.

"It doesn't look like he has any more information after all," my husband said after checking with the nurse. "You're being discharged. Once you've gotten dressed, we can go."

****

It was because of how dire my "disturbances" felt from the inside that every time a doctor seemed to have dismissed my cries for help as nothing more than the ranting of a menopausal woman or a hysterical hypochondriac, I would become even more determined to find someone who would take me seriously. This time, however, certain I had exhausted all of my options, instead of rushing off to some new doctor or to some other ER, the next day I did my best to try to settle back into my old life, my old life with the new me—the mad-woman me—still vying for top billing.

I can remember standing in the kitchen that next morning, trying to bake cookies and make something for lunch while my sons stood behind me, both of them excitedly telling me about their week at school. Although this had been a typical morning activity in our house for nearly a decade, suddenly it felt as if I'd never made cookies before, as if I'd never held a mixing spoon or been in my own kitchen before, and that my sons were speaking in riddles. No matter how hard I tried, I couldn't follow what my sons were saying, and, even worse, I couldn't grab hold of anything they were saying long enough to try to follow it. Everything around me seemed to be shifting now, not smoothly but with all of these jagged stops and starts, sort of like a broken conveyor belt that keeps stopping and then snapping back into motion, throwing everything on it into a confused heap on the floor. As I continued to try and make sense of my sons' excited tales and of where the cookies needed to go on the cookie sheet, every now and then that image of a woman walking into the lake would suddenly pop into my mind, and keep popping in until, somehow, I'd manage to blink her away.

I have to be able to do this, I thought. *I have to be able to stay sane…to stay focused on my life and on my sons.*

But even with these determined and hopeful mantras, ever since my visit to the hospital the day before, something else inside of me seemed to have snapped, something that left me teetering all the more closer to the edge. At least in the beginning of my crisis, there were avenues I could take to try to help myself, doctors I could see and illnesses I could research… hopes I could hold onto. Now, there was nothing, nothing but trying to live with the madness, trying to make sense of the madness, and, worst of all, trying to fall sleep with the madness once darkness came.

Why can't I sleep? I wondered later that night, as I lay wide-awake on the living room floor. *Please God, please help me fall sleep.*

As I continued tossing and turning, it began to feel as if all the walls in the house were closing in on me, leaning in closer and closer, making it hard for me to breathe. I must have sat up and laid back down at least ten times to try to catch my breath, maybe more. Finally, sometime around 2 a.m. or so, out of my mind with frustration, I balled my hand up into fist and tried to push it into my mouth and down my throat. Was it to try to kill myself or just to see if I could? When I realized how ridiculous this was, even more frustrated, I slammed my head against the cold-carpeted floor. That was it.

Desperate to escape the stifling air of the living room and, even more, the stifling air inside my head, I got up off the floor. It was the middle of the night. I knew where the lake was. It was only a mile or so from my house, and, certainly, by the time I got there, that woman would be there too, that woman I kept seeing in my mind's eye, that part of me who so wanted to die. But there were other parts of me too, other parts of me that wanted to live, that needed to live. Which woman was I supposed to be, damn it? Which one? Not knowing what else to do and terrified by what I might do, I went into the bedroom and crawled onto the edge of the bed.

"Are you okay?" my husband asked as he rolled over to look at me.

I wasn't okay. I hadn't been okay for months, for years. I knew that. Now it was time I acknowledged something even more painful.

"I just want to die," I moaned, pushing my head into the mattress. "I just want to die. Oh, please. Oh, please. I just want to die."

Although I can't remember what happened then (did I lie down on the bed or did I go back to wandering around the house?), I do remember that when morning came, I hadn't gotten even a minute of sleep. With so many other sleepless nights already behind me, my state of mind was growing shakier by the minute. And yet, as if on auto-pilot, as soon as I heard the alarm I got myself dressed and started plowing around the house—feeding the dog, feeding the cat, getting breakfast ready, all the while hoping that, at some point, everything would start to feel normal.

Still running on autopilot, once I finished dropping my sons off at school, I took my dog for a walk and came home to start my yoga practice. On my way into my room, I was surprised to see my husband already out of bed, sitting in his office making phone calls.

Isn't it too early for that? I wondered. *Too early for him to be working already?*

With the bustle of the morning nearly over, I could feel the sleeplessness of the night beginning to catch up with me, pulling me into slow motion and into even more confusion and fear, pulling me into remembering some of the night's most agonizing moments.

Did I really tell my husband I wanted to die? I asked myself. *And if I did, did I really mean it? Do I really want to die?*

I could hear the hum of the refrigerator and my husband still talking on the phone. For a moment, I thought I heard him mention my name.

"...Lynda...that's what she said...yeah, last night..."

Although I'm not sure whether it was by my overhearing more of his conversation or him finally telling me, a few minutes later I learned that the reason for my husband's early morning phone calls didn't have anything to do with his job. The reason he was on the phone so early was to arrange for me to go to a psychiatric hospital, to arrange for me to go there because of the thoughts I was having about suicide. But was I really suicidal? Was I? Or was I just out of my mind with frustration? Whatever my feelings were, I knew my husband's history with such things wasn't an easy one. With a father who committed suicide at only forty-eight years-old, he knew the horrors of having someone snatched away by their own hand all too well, much too well, I'm sure, to sit by and wait to see whether my late night plea was a valid one.

"We'll just go take a look at the place," my husband said as he brought up a picture of the hospital on the internet. "If you don't like it you don't have to stay, but we have to do something."

"When do I have to go?" I asked, eyeing the photo.

"I'm waiting for the hospital to call back so they can tell us when they'll have a bed available," my husband replied. "We should know in a little while."

I could hardly believe how quickly everything was happening. Here I'd been trying for months to get myself admitted to a hospital, any hospital, and now it was all just falling into my lap. Was this the best thing for me? The worst thing? Did I still want to go? Before I could even locate these

questions inside my mind, the phone rang. It was someone
from the hospital calling to say that a bed had just opened up
and that they would be able to admit me later that afternoon.

As soon as I was able to grasp the reality of where I was
going and when, my mind shot into overdrive. There were still
so many things I needed to take care of at home. How would
I ever get to all of them? Leaving my husband to continue
talking to the nurse, the first thing I did was hurry outside
to mow the lawn. That's right, mow the lawn. With how
obsessive I was about taking care of the house, this seemed to
make perfect sense. What if I wasn't able to come home for a
long time? What if I never came home? To be honest, I don't
have any idea what I was thinking when I climbed onto the
tractor that morning, or even if I was thinking. All I know is
that, as usual, I had to keep moving.

Even before I finished the lawn, my mind was already
racing ahead to what needed to be done next—the laundry, the
vacuuming, my yoga. My yoga! Realizing that I hadn't done
my yoga yet, as soon as I put the tractor away I took a shower
and then hurried out onto the sun-porch. Determined to get
through my practice regardless of my state of mind, once I
rolled my mat out across the floor, I turned on my CD player
and began moving through my daily postures.

Sun Salutations. Warrior I. Warrior II…

It was while I was hovering between one Warrior posture
and another that I began to notice something strange about the
music playing on the CD player. For some reason, every song
had begun to sound exactly the same. No matter how long the
CD continued to play and no matter how many different songs
I should have heard come through the speakers, all the songs
sounded alike. I tried pushing the "track change" button to

see if that would fix it. Still no change, so I tried pushing the button again, and again, and again.

Why do all the songs sound the same?

Not knowing what else to do, I tried shutting the CD player off and then turning it back on to see if that would change the song, but still, all I could hear were those same droning notes.

Isn't this the same song as the last one? I thought nervously. *Isn't this the same song as the last song and the song before that?*

Push a button. Push a button.

Why doesn't the song ever change?

It was while I was pushing all the buttons that I started having these flashes, visions that I was going to storm into the house and start pummeling my husband, that I was going to kick him, punch him, scratch him, tear his eyes out… something. Much like my suicidal thoughts, these visions didn't seem to be coming from me but from some other part of me, some deep, rage-filled part of me I couldn't fully connect to. It was as if someone was playing a movie inside my head, a movie I'd never even heard of.

Why am I having these thoughts? I wondered, the images still racing through my mind. *I must really be crazy! I must have really lost my mind! They're going to put me away forever. I just know it! They're going to put me away forever!*

"Someone from the hospital wants to talk to you."

Although I hadn't heard him come in, I looked up to see my husband there on the porch, reaching out to hand me the phone. Shutting off the CD player, I put the phone up to my ear and felt my visions of violence slip quietly into the background.

"…Clean linens will be provided," I can remember the nurse saying, "but you'll need to bring three days' worth of clothes with you and whatever toiletry items you think you might need. Does that sound manageable?"

"Yes, it does," I replied.

"Do you have any questions?" the nurse asked.

"No. No, I don't think so."

As soon as I hung up the phone, I went into my room and started packing the things the nurse said I should bring, still struggling to come to terms with where I was going and, even more, with what I was leaving behind.

I've never left my dog overnight before, I worried, *and I'm rarely away from my sons. What am I going to do without them? What are they going to do without me?*

After tucking my journal into my suitcase, I went out to the kitchen to pack my vitamins, the bottles and bottles of vitamins I felt I needed to stay alive, so many bottles that I had to pack them separately in a plastic bag.

"There's another phone call for you," I heard my husband say as he came up behind me. "It's Dr. S."

Even as I was reaching for the phone, I wasn't all that sure I wanted to talk to Dr. S. When I'd seen him just a few days earlier, he seemed so convinced that it was some sort of physical malady causing my "disturbances." Now, with all the talk about suicide and psychiatric hospitals, he was bound to believe otherwise. Embarrassed, I took the phone and went back into my room.

"I'm afraid they're not going to let me come home," I told Dr. S. "What if I'm so crazy they don't let me come home?"

"Of course you'll come home," Dr. S. replied, his voice as calm as always. "Feel free to call me anytime while you're there. I'd be more than happy to speak with you."

But not even Dr. S. and his calm voice could comfort me now. It felt like I was airborne and crashing down to earth all at the same time. For reasons that no doctor seemed to be able to figure out, I had lost my mind, and, in just a few hours would be committing myself to a psychiatric hospital—and I still had to tell my sons.

I went to the school to pick David and Jonathan up at 2:30 like I always did, and then waited until they were both in the car to tell them what was happening.

"I have to go to a psychiatric hospital," I said, trying hard to make it sound less frightening than it was, less final than it felt.

"What? David asked. "Why? When?"

"I have to go today," I replied, "as soon as we get home."

In the long moment of silence that hung over the car, I could feel my whole world crumbling around me, and my sons' world crumbling in on top of it.

"Today?" Jonathan exclaimed. "What do you mean? What about the Sjogren's Syndrome? What about…"

"Couldn't we try to find another doctor?" David asked. "Someone who could…"

Even though I did still believe that it was Sjogren's Syndrome and Cerebral Vasculitis causing at least some my "disturbances," I knew that didn't matter now, certainly not as much as that woman who kept trying to get to the lake.

"I have no choice," I said firmly. "I have to go."

Worried about whether there would be enough food at home while I was gone, after leaving the school I stopped at a nearby market to pick up some essentials—potato chips, eggs, bread, and carrots—and then we all went home. There, I explained as best as I could and as quickly as I could about managing the household—what the dog needed and when, what the cat needed, the carpets, the toilet, the washing machine. When I got to the end of my list, it felt as if all the air had suddenly been sucked out of the room.

"I don't understand why you have to go," Jonathan said as I put on my coat. "I don't understand."

Torn between knowing I had no choice but to go and yet so wanting to stay with my sons, I turned to look at my reflection in the hallway mirror. More than anything, I hoped to see someone I could recognize gazing back at me, but found my eyes looking just as emotionless, just as flat as the day I stood in the hallway closet. Grabbing a flashlight out of the kitchen drawer, I aimed it toward my eyes and turned to face my sons.

"Can't you see it?" I demanded as I switched the flashlight on and off. "Can't you see how dead my eyes look, how my pupils don't even dilate anymore?"

My sons stepped forward and began searching my eyes.

"Oh, yeah, I do see it," Jonathan said slowly, his voice low and sad. "They look like all the color's gone out of them, all the life."

After setting the flashlight down on the counter, I leaned over to pick up my suitcase.

"Mom, please," my sons begged as I started out the door. "Mom, please…don't go. What are we going to do here without you? Mom, please!"

I hesitated for no more than a second or two to look back at my sons' frightened faces, and then stepped outside into the late afternoon sunlight.

Will I ever come home again? I wondered as I got into the car. *Will I ever be sane enough to come home again?*

For the full two hours it took to drive to the psychiatric hospital, I sat in the car next to my husband, barely saying a word. There wasn't anything I could say, nothing that could change anything now. The beast had completely taken over, and, in my madness, I had become his hostage.

The Next Chapter...

Menopause in Crisis— The Journey Home

AFTER NOTES

Before we part, I feel it is important for me to point out that my intention in including the information related to my childhood abuse in this memoir is not to accuse or defame any particular person or persons as being the perpetrator(s) of that abuse. My only objective is to offer as clear a picture as possible about the events that led up to my crisis, as well as to help women with similar histories and similar menopausal challenges gain a better understanding of what they may be going through.

Please also note that another version of this memoir was submitted as the Culminating Project for my MA degree and is now included in the university library under a different title and author last name. (All first names used in the memoir have been kept intact.)

Acknowledgements and sincere thanks to...

~Raye M., whose encouragement and insights offered me the support I needed to weave this chaotic time in my life into a cohesive story.

~Linda E., whose editorial advice and ability to ask the right questions inspired me to look more closely.

~Barbara B., DC, for the adjustments that kept my "writer's neck" in line throughout this writing and for lending an ear as the story unfolded.

~Scarlett R., for the creativity and know-how that helped me to transform these words from a manuscript into a publishable book.

~Marguerite H., for being there when the chips were down.

~Robin O., for the nudge that helped me to take the next step.

~my mystical writing guides, the man in the white turban and the elder woman, whose wise counsel in my writing continues to astound me.

~all the people who touched my life during my crisis—doctors and nurses, friends and neighbors, husbands and ex-husbands—as each one played a part in shaping the events that created this memoir.

~my parents, for the good times and the bad for even the bad times have added texture and meaning to my life.

~Dr. S., for the wisdom and compassion that helped me find my way to a place of sanity and truth.

~and finally, to the two people who have been the most instrumental in helping me bring this memoir to life, and who stand as a constant source of love, encouragement, and inspiration in all of my endeavors—my sons, David and Jonathan. If not for the generous compassion of these kind souls, I don't know if I would have ever found my way back from the brink. The laughter and friendship they have brought to my life are truly the brightest lights on my path.

Resources

Barbach, Lonnie, PhD. *The Pause, Positive Approaches to Perimenopause and Menopause.* 2nd. New York: Penguin, 2000. Print.

Bass, Ellen, and Laura Davis. *The Courage to Heal--A Guide for Women Survivors of Child Sexual Abuse.* 3rd. New York: HarperCollins, 1994. Print.

Kostrubala, Thaddeus. *The Joy of Running.* 4th. New York: Lippincott, 1976. 130-131. Print.

"Schizophrenia." www.*Athealth.com.* Mental Health: A Report of the Surgeon General December 1999, n.d. Web. 22 Jul 2013.

"34 Menopause Symptoms." *http://www.34-menopause-symptoms.com/.* 34 Menopause Symptoms, n.d. Web. 22 Jul 2013.

"What is a Dissociative Disorder." *www.Sidran.org.* Sidran.org, 2010. Web. 22 Jul 2013.

*Side effects for medications retrieved from www.drugs.com and www.rxlist.com

.

Made in the USA
Charleston, SC
05 November 2013